Wrigleyworld

A Season
in Baseball's
Best
Neighborhood

Kevin Kaduk

 NEW AMERICAN LIBRARY

New American Library
Published by New American Library, a division of
Penguin Group (USA) Inc., 375 Hudson Street,
New York, New York 10014, USA
Penguin Group (Canada), 90 Eglinton Avenue East, Suite 700, Toronto,
Ontario M4P 2Y3, Canada (a division of Pearson Penguin Canada Inc.)
Penguin Books Ltd., 80 Strand, London WC2R 0RL, England
Penguin Ireland, 25 St. Stephen's Green, Dublin 2,
Ireland (a division of Penguin Books Ltd.)
Penguin Group (Australia), 250 Camberwell Road, Camberwell, Victoria 3124,
Australia (a division of Pearson Australia Group Pty. Ltd.)
Penguin Books India Pvt. Ltd., 11 Community Centre, Panchsheel Park,
New Delhi - 110 017, India
Penguin Group (NZ), cnr Airborne and Rosedale Roads, Albany,
Auckland 1310, New Zealand (a division of Pearson New Zealand Ltd.)
Penguin Books (South Africa) (Pty.) Ltd., 24 Sturdee Avenue,
Rosebank, Johannesburg 2196, South Africa

Penguin Books Ltd., Registered Offices:
80 Strand, London WC2R 0RL, England

First published by New American Library,
a division of Penguin Group (USA) Inc.

First Printing, April 2006
10   9   8   7   6   5   4   3   2   1

Copyright © Kevin Kaduk, 2006
Map by G. W. Ward
All rights reserved

 REGISTERED TRADEMARK—MARCA REGISTRADA

LIBRARY OF CONGRESS CATALOGING-IN-PUBLICATION DATA:

Kaduk, Kevin.
Wrigleyworld:a season in baseball's best neighborhood/Kevin Kaduk.
    p.   cm.
ISBN 0-451-21812-4 (hardcover)
    1. Wrigley Field (Chicago, Ill.).   2. Chicago Cubs (Baseball team).   3. Stadiums—Social
aspects—Illinois—Chicago.   I. Title.
GV416.I32K34   2006   2005029700

Set in Berkeley Medium
Design by Ginger Legato

Printed in the United States of America

PUBLISHER'S NOTE
While the author has made every effort to provide accurate telephone numbers and Internet addresses
at the time of publication, neither the publisher nor the author assumes any responsibility for errors,
or for changes that occur after publication. Further, publisher does not have any control over and does
not assume any responsibility for author or third-party Web sites or their content.

For Mom, Dad, Dave and Kris—
the best bullpen around

"Eighty-five percent of the world is working. The other fifteen come out here to watch day baseball."

—Lee Elia, Chicago Cubs manager, 1983

"Wrigley is like another home in the community—when you're in Wrigley Field, it's like you're visiting the family of all the people that live around there." —Ernie Banks

"Booze, broads, and bullshit—if you've got that, what else do you need?" —Harry Caray

1. Main entrance/Wrigley Field: Home of Chicago Cubs sign
2. Harry Caray statue
3. Wrigleyville's Engine 78
4. Waveland and Kenmore—stakeout spot for Ballhawks
5. Murphy's Bleachers
6. 3627 Sheffield—Will's apartment/first rooftop visited
7. 3633 Sheffield—Lake View Baseball Club/second rooftop visited
8. Bleacher entrance
9. McDonald's
10. Players' parking lot/proposed site for parking garage/Cubs museum
11. Cubby Bear
12. Sluggers
13. John Barleycorn
14. Sports Corner
15. CTA El Station, Red Line
16. Taco Bell
17. 7-Eleven
18. Hi-Tops
19. Casey Moran's
20. Bernie's Tap
21. Wrigley Field vendor staging area
22. The Full Shilling
23. Goose Island
24. Third row/bleachers—preferred-seating spot
25. Aisle 4—site of the "Bartman Incident"
26. Scalper Alley
27. Landing spot of Sammy Sosa's 536-foot home run in 2003
28. The "Budweiser" house

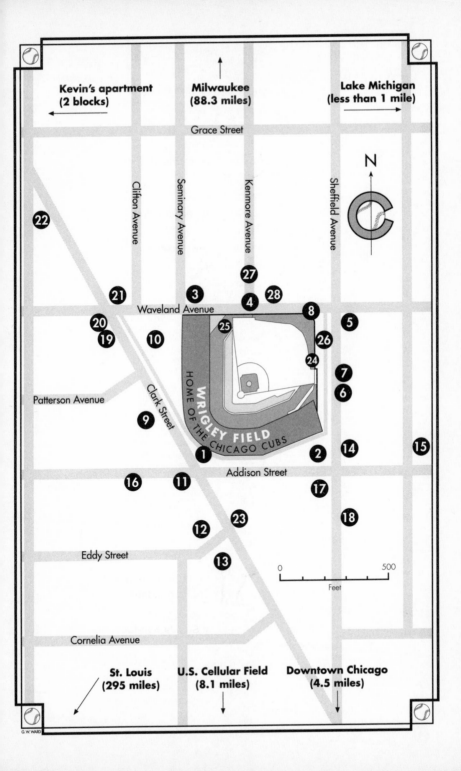

Wrigleyworld

Introduction

Sweet Home, Chicago

Everyone has a story about moving to Wrigleyville, and this is mine: After I'd spent three years in Kansas City, the phone calls became a regular occurrence, arriving on sunny, weekend afternoons, when I was escaping the oppressive sun with a blasting air conditioner and a Cubs game on WGN.

I'd be doing nothing in particular (though maybe taking a nap), when my cell phone would buzz and a wall of crowd noise would greet my answer. Everyone bitches about these people on their phones at baseball games, but we've all done it at one point or another. It's too big a temptation. When I was living away from Chicago, it seemed like my friends happened to do it more than most.

"You'll never guess where I'm at," one of the guys would invariably yell in an Old Style–drenched voice. "I mean, *you'll never guess where I'm at*."

It wasn't hard to deduce. In the spirit of *rubbingmynoseinit* (German for "I'm here and you're not"), my friends were calling from Wrigley. A pause was essential in responding; maybe they'd grow confused and hang up. Sometimes I was forced to respond.

So I'd let loose a diatribe that they usually couldn't hear above the crowd noise.

"Well, based on your drunk dial from last week's Cubs-Braves game, I'm going to guess you're at Wrigley Field," I'd say. "Or is that too obvious of a choice? Maybe you're at a motocross rally? If so, that's funny, because I don't hear any engines."

This would inevitably be followed by a surge of cheers.

"Wait . . . *what?* I can't hear you. I think Sammy just went yard but I can't see. We're going nuts here. I'll call you later."

More crowd noise as my friend searched for the END button. Then, *click.* I'd be left alone, watching Sosa circle the bases on WGN.

"I should be there," I'd think.

I had grown accustomed to following the fun from afar. The Cubs were often on WGN, the Chicago-based superstation carried by cable systems across the country, including in Kansas City. If the game wasn't televised, there was always the surprisingly clear feed on mlb.com. In the morning, checking the *Sun-Times* and *Tribune* Web sites came before putting on pants.

I came to learn there was a special dynamic when watching a Cubs game from a different city. After years of heading to Wrigley in person, it was possible to watch the games with a unique perspective. The WGN cameras focused on their usual targets: the players in the infield, the ivy on the outfield walls, the old ladies wearing funny hats in the grandstands. But with my firsthand knowledge of the park, my memory was able to fill in everything not on-screen: the 7-Eleven on Sheffield Avenue where we bought pocket flasks of Captain Morgan and dumped them into Big Gulps, the free parking places on Lakewood or Cornelia, the pizza place "up the stairs" on Addison.

Because I was battling an on-again, off-again case of homesickness, these sensory-infused broadcasts (along with reruns of

The Real World: Chicago) proved to be a valuable antidote to my pangs for the Windy City.

In a weird way, I was able to take the broadcast and project myself into Wrigleyville for a couple of hours. Without seeing him, I knew superfan Ronnie "Woo-Woo" Wickers was there, cheering the Cubs in his trademark full uniform. I knew that some of my friends were prowling the streets outside, waiting for the scalpers' prices to crash an inning into the game. I knew what half of the crowd would be doing after—an afternoon of beers on the patio of Sports Corner while bikini-topped girls paraded by.

This vicarious approach worked for a while. But my first year in Kansas City passed, then my second. Watching on television wasn't enough anymore.

As my friends called from the park, I grew increasingly jealous. One day, a friend texted a message saying he was in the bleachers. I responded by typing "screw off" into my cell phone. "You OK man?" he wrote back later.

Another time, I got a call from a friend who lived two blocks from Wrigley. He was sitting down the right field line, within heckling distance of the visitors' bullpen. Two good-looking girls—at least he *said* they were good-looking—were sitting on either side of him.

"Craziest thing, dude," he said. "We were sitting in our front yard, drinking beers, when these two girls walk up. They've got two extra tickets and want to know if we want to go to the game with them. So we had a few beers before heading over to the park. Now they want us to go party with some of their friends after the game."

He then delivered the final blow: "Man, you should really be here right now."

October 2003 came and the Cubs reached the brink of achieving the impossible, jumping to a 3–2 lead over the Florida Marlins in the National League Championship Series. The newspaper I was working for, the *Kansas City Star*, sent me to cover the scene for games six and (if necessary) seven at Wrigley. Ten minutes after Steve Bartman achieved infamy by reaching for a foul ball in game six, I was in Aisle Four, being doused by some of the beer intended for the overeager and bespectacled Cubs fan.

Despite the strange pride I took in being a chronicler of a classic heartbreak (the Cubs obviously fell in game seven), the taste of Wrigleyville during the playoffs proved to be too much to bear. I yearned to be back in Chicago. The temptation to return grew larger in 2004, when the Cubs, favored by most in the sports media to reach the Series, contended up until the final week of the season before suffering their inevitable implosion.

By late 2004, I found myself entering a fourth year in Kansas City, still climbing the journalistic career ladder, primarily by covering prep sports on the Kansas side of the state line. It was a sometimes mind-numbing task that involved talking to (1) proud but hyperactive parents, (2) overworked and underpaid coaches, and (3) teenage athletes with little to say (sample interview response: *"You know what's awesome? Clothes from Hollister"*).

While my superiors were encouraging and I worked my way into better stories, my singular end goal—nabbing a sportswriting job back home in the Windy City—never stopped calling. Eventually I became impatient with the dues-paying tactics of stalking the sidelines at rainy prep football games or freezing on metal bleachers at softball games in March. When I was passed over for a promotion opportunity at the *Star*, my editor suggested a few more years on the high school beat. I was going places, he told me. Just not at the moment.

To me, "a few more years" in Kansas City sounded like a denial for parole. After the talk with my boss, a quote came to mind: "The Cubs are for everyone who ever said 'no' to their boss," said Bill Veeck, the man who planted ivy on the walls of Wrigley.

Suddenly, that statement seemed like more than just a witty quote. It was a damn good idea.

With the quote in mind, I again met with my editor in early December. He wanted to gauge my interest in that oxymoronic concept of a more prestigious prep job. Thanks, but no, thanks, I said. He wanted to know what I would do instead.

"I think I might go back to Chicago," I said. "Follow the Cubs."

"You going to try for a job at a paper up there?"

"Nah, nothing like that. I'm just going to watch baseball. You know, drink some beers, have some fun."

And, like that, I had done what countless others had surely dreamed of doing. I up and left an *actual* job with *actual* benefits, an *actual* 401(k), and *actual* exposure to 250,000 *actual* readers to follow a baseball team that hadn't won a World Series title in the past ninety-seven years (and counting).

With a malnourished bank account and a half-assed idea to do some freelancing, I planned a move to Wrigleyville, intent on having the type of summer that any twenty-six-year-old male would want.

From the outset, I knew I had some missions to tackle. Jousting with scalpers on a daily basis. Drinking all-you-can-drink beer and eating all-you-can-eat bratwurst on the Waveland and Sheffield rooftops. Closing out bars by sharing shots of tequila with recent graduates (preferably female, preferably large-chested) from the University of Indiana.

Most important, I wanted to know about the neighborhood. I wanted to understand how it became a living, breathing thing, a circus, a spectacle on game days. I wanted to find out how it felt when the Cubs were away on a nine-game West Coast swing. I wanted to be there 24/7, walking home from the bars as the groundskeepers were showing up for their morning routine.

Wrigleyville would be my home for a season. I would be living a life that many thought impossible. Each day, those same people would sit in downtown high-rises, dreaming up medical maladies and personal tragedies so they could ditch their jobs for an afternoon date against the Giants.

Now the only bonds I knew about were Barry and Bobby. When my friends learned of the plan, they jealously shook their heads and expressed their doubts. One called it a "harebrained scheme," another said he had friends who wished they were me.

"What you're describing truly sounds like one of the greatest ideas of all time," a friend wrote one day. "For your next adventure, I might suggest examining 1,500 Las Vegas showgirls to find out if they're real or fake."

It wasn't a bad idea. But first there was a season of baseball to watch. As I drove the moving truck back to Chicago I liked to think that Harry Caray was somewhere up above, raising a can of Bud at the precise moment I left my job in Kansas City.

"Holy Cow!" he was saying.

Frequently Asked Questions

April

Q: *This idea to just watch baseball for a season seems impulsive and, might I say, a little immature. You're twenty-six years old. Shouldn't you be building a career or, you know, maybe trying to meet a girl and start a family?*

A: This may sound silly, irresponsible, or both, but, four years out of college, I have already become very tired of working. It really isn't for me. I need to take a break.

Going to baseball games seems like something I'd do in retirement. Why not speed up the process?

Since my baseball career peaked when I hit a walk-off RBI double in the last game of Pony League, being a spectator is the only way to be involved with the game from this point on.

(I suppose I could also become a hot dog vendor, but I once had an unfortunate incident with tin foil.)

Q: *Last season I went to Wrigley and they wanted $100 for a seat in the bleachers. You don't have season tickets, and the entire season practically sold out within three days in February. How the hell are you going to get into games?*

A: How little you know me. Over the course of my life, I have probably attended in excess of seven hundred sporting events. I would guess that I've picked up tickets on the street for at least 75 percent of them.

Quite simply, bartering with (and the eventual defeat of) scalpers may be my simplest pleasure in life. I learned it from Dad, whom I'm sure could somehow find a ticket for the Second Coming. Naturally, he'd get in for under face.

Q: *Wait, what happened with the tin foil?*
A: To make a long story short, there was a German shepherd and an electrical outlet. I refuse to discuss it further.

Q: *Baseball is boring. Are you really going to sit through eighty-one games?*
A: There's a T-shirt that people wear around Wrigleyville. It reads, "Baseball isn't boring. You are." But to answer your question: No, I won't be at every game that is played at Wrigley this year.

That's what happens when you buy a high-definition television and WGN's picture quality ranks better than the view from the Cubs dugout.

Kidding aside, I'm going to try and approach this as any fan would. When I feel like going to a baseball game, I'll ramble over to Wrigley and try to pick up a ticket. When that doesn't happen, I'll just hang out, watch crowds and talk to people. I am nothing if not a fan of spectacle.

Q: *I assume that your diet will consist primarily of beer and hot dogs. How do you plan to keep your weight below three hundred pounds?*
A: To be fair, my meals will be varied. I also plan to eat a metric ton of peanuts, several hundred ballpark pretzels, and an occasional pepperoni-and-mushroom pizza from Lou Malnati's (with the buttercrust, of course).

Q: *This whole plan is a lifelong dream, isn't it?*
A: Yes. When I was younger, I used to look at the apartment buildings on Waveland and Sheffield and wonder what it would be like to live there.

Truthfully, I have always wanted to live near *any* stadium. When Dad took me to see the Bulls at Chicago Stadium, eight-year-olds from the projects would come and clean our windshield after the game. Then Dad would give them each a dollar and they'd move to the next car.

These kids were freezing to make a buck. Yet all I could think was, *Man, they're so lucky to live down here.* I imagined they went to every game and watched Michael Jordan every night.

That they probably couldn't afford one Bulls game, let alone an entire season ticket package, never entered my preteen mind.

Q: *Remember when you had a framed picture of former Cubs first baseman Leon Durham hanging on your bedroom wall in college and you told that girl (you know the one I mean) that Leon was your adopted brother?*
A: Vaguely. But I think alcohol was involved.

Q: *This isn't going to be a typical Cubs book, is it?*
A: Did you just figure that out? Bookstores and libraries are packed with books about the Cubs, their curse, and "beautiful Wrigley Field." It's admittedly impossible to escape some of the clichés when you're talking about sports, and especially the Cubs. But this is a book about what it means to be a twenty-something baseball fan in

Wrigleyville. Sometimes that involves booze and women. In other words, George Will probably isn't going to like it.

Q: *Are the Cubs going to win the World Series this year?*
A: To quote the best sports song this side of the Notre Dame Victory March, *"Hey, hey, holy mackerel . . . No doubt about it . . . The Cubs are on their way."* But that's what we sing in Chicago every year.

Chapter One

Beer Springs Eternal

Friday, April 8—vs. Milwaukee

The season's first glimpse of Wrigley comes as I walk north on Sheffield Avenue. For some reason, the following actions seem appropriate: a pumping of the fist, kissing the brick on the right field wall, or maybe releasing a fax like Jordan did for his return to the NBA in 1995.

"I'm back," it would say.

I *am* back. After three years in baseball purgatory, defined as wherever the Royals happen to be playing, I have returned to the corner of Clark and Addison, a.k.a. the Friendly Confines, home of the Chicago Cubs.

In 2003, I attended five games here. In 2004, none. Those totals will be crushed this season. Each Cubs home game is available to me, live and in the flesh. On May 1, I'll move to a place that is a five-minute walk (four blocks) from the corner of Waveland and Clark. Until then, I'm crashing on a couch in Lincoln Park, a five-minute ride from Wrigley on the CTA's Red Line.

I am looking at a Cubs pocket schedule, the kind they give out at the counter at Osco Drug. There are eighty-one dates laid out on a calendar grid, each containing the team names that seem brash yet attractive in their abbreviated form—STL, PIT,

CIN. To baseball fans, these schedules appear poetic. Spread across five months, the campaign seems limitless.

Standing outside the right field wall and looking at the Wrigley Field scoreboard (it is 5:45 a.m.* and the day's matchups have already been posted), I think about the requirements of surviving a baseball season. Whether you're a player, a manager, a GM, or even a fan, an entire campaign mandates a certain amount of patience and endurance. In return, you receive sustained hope, or, if you live somewhere like Tampa Bay or Detroit, extended misery.

Baseball is the male soap opera, though such a label overlooks the number of women who follow the sport. It is a pin-striped *Days of our Lives*, with the heroes and villains changing on a more frequent basis. A dissection of the characters and events arrives on our front doorsteps each morning. Hours later, there's a new episode for our consumption.

If the Cubs weren't coming off back-to-back winning seasons, I might not be here. Back-to-back winning seasons? There's a situation I can't resolve in my head.

This new alliterative premise—Cubs as consistent contenders—has a strange fit. Back in the day (and by that I mean 1997) we always thought this might be the year for the Cubs. But like a father at a screeching fourth-grade orchestra concert, we really didn't have a reason to believe in our support. We were just trying to be nice.

Now the Cubs are giving us a little reason to believe. This year's payroll is $87 million, among the highest in the league. The team's top four starters—Mark Prior, Kerry Wood, Carlos Zambrano, and Greg Maddux—seem to be impenetrable, if only they can stay healthy. Sammy Sosa has been traded to Baltimore,

*Despite not being able to sell alcohol until seven in the morning, most Wrigleyville bars have opened by quarter to six. Only on Opening Day in Wrigleyville would this make complete sense.

taking his declining power numbers and salsa-blaring boom box with him.

But this being Wrigleyville, there are also reasons for pessimism. The team dropped two of three games in Arizona to start the season. General manager Jim Hendry did nothing to address the anemic bullpen, instead calling on unreliable LaTroy Hawkins for another season. The team didn't re-sign Moises Alou in left field, leaving us to pin our hopes on . . . Jason Dubois and Todd Hollandsworth? (Sigh.)

When I arrive at Wrigley this morning, I am wearing a long-sleeve T-shirt, a heavy pullover and a blue North Face fleece. A few hours later, I start to sweat. I remove the fleece and tie it around my waist. There is power in layers.

The temperature is approaching the sixties. It's not warm by Florida standards, but that's all we can ask for. On Sheffield Avenue, more than a hundred people have already lined up along the right field fence. I am one of them, though I've yet to find a ticket.

Sweating on Opening Day. In Chicago, the first day of the baseball season is not supposed to involve heat. Instead, we huddle in the green stands at Wrigley Field, chasing cold beers with hot chocolates. We bring heavy blankets and woolly scarves and hats and gloves left over from Bears season. If we could sneak them in under our jackets, we'd bring in cookstoves and space heaters, too.

Everyone sees Wrigley as this summer party place, where guys are perpetually shirtless and girls show up wearing only bikini tops. That's only part of the truth. Wrigley is also about freezing your ass off in April. The cold, we like to say in Chicago, builds character.

My stunt is about more than just watching baseball. I'm also here for everything else that goes with living in Wrigleyville. While it's true that Chicago sportswriters have been calling Wrigley "the world's largest outdoor beer garden" since the '60s, the place has taken more of a party-bent approach in recent years (and this is saying something). In 2003, when the Cubs charged toward the National League Central title, overflow crowds swarmed the neighborhood for each home game, looking for an extra ticket or, at the very least, a spot near the front of the bar.

The party carried over to the 2004 opener and charged its way through the disappointing final weekend. People from all walks of life—frat boys, sorority sisters, punks, Goths, nerds, businessmen, families, the elderly—all came together to support what was supposed to be another extended run at the elusive World Series. When that didn't happen, everyone just ordered another round.

Now the game day experience has become more than just a few beers with your friends before heading home. This is Mardi Gras for the Midwest, complete with live music and flashes of what the French call *le boob*.

Don't have a ticket to the game? Don't worry! Just sit in a bar and spend your money on beers priced the same as in the ballpark. Last year, so many people came to Wrigleyville with this plan that a hyperbolic columnist predicted Armageddon.

A lot of the bandwagon jumpers don't even seem to notice that a Major League Baseball team plays here. For example, take my first bar visit of the season:

At six this morning, I entered Hi-Tops, located across from the right field entrance on Sheffield. On the stage stood a goateed Chicago shock jock and his posse. In front, a crowd of twenty-somethings, most of them wearing hard-ass black, paid close attention. Everyone seemed to be having a good time, so I craned my neck to see what I was missing.

Two men were pouring lighter fluid on their testicles.

For some reason (and Lord knows why), I wasn't fazed. Seconds later, a flame was lit, causing each man to dance around for what were presumably a few uncomfortable seconds. The crowd squirmed, then roared. A few fans with video cameras pushed closer toward the stage.

The gross-out contest continued for two more steps, the details of which I am hesitant to reveal here. (However, I will tell you it involved the following: strippers, peanut butter, and vomit.) When one of the men left the stage, a swarm of questions went through my mind.

Were Opening Day tickets at stake? Would you like some aloe for, uh, your . . . uh, err . . . you know . . . your [points toward crotch]? *What in the name of Durocher is wrong with you?*

Instead, I went with a simple: "Why would you do something like that?"

"I just love life, man," said the obviously drunk contestant, before immediately heading to the bathroom.

And, truly, what expresses a love for life more than a flaming nut sack?

Over the next two hours, a number of odd things happened at Hi-Tops. Among them: A gaggle of strippers from a competing club made its way through the door, creating a tense atmosphere with the exotics already on hand. (Or perhaps I just imagined it that way.) A group of midgets performed a few songs, dressed as the members of KISS. After that, another set of little people took the stage. Their main act was to hit each other with metal objects like cheese graters. Then a one-eyed man took the stage and poured a cup of beer through his empty eye socket, causing it to come back through his mouth.

That another season of Wrigley Field baseball would begin in a few hours seemed only coincidental. Forget about ceremonial first pitches and notions like hope springs eternal. When it comes to the Wrigleyville bars, Opening Day takes on an entirely different connotation.

After taking in the debauchery at Hi-Tops, I headed toward Yak-zies on Clark, where WXRT was throwing an Opening Day concert featuring Widespread Panic and the Waco Brothers. Billy Corgan, the lead singer of the Smashing Pumpkins and noted Chicago sports fan, was supposed to show. When I was there, I squeezed into the beer tent between a group of forty-somethings from Algonquin and a Panic fan named Mark, whose fanaticism for the band was surpassed only by his passion for not using soap. Perhaps it was the early hour, but I could swear that patchouli-powered stink lines were emanating from his hemp poncho.

"All these people, they're here for Panic?" asked Mark through a hazy pair of bloodshot eyes. "I mean, they're here for Panic *this early in the morning?*"

"Nah, most people are here for the Cubs opener."

"The what?" Mark asked back.

"Never mind."

Later, Mark got down on his knees, scrunched up against a bench, and immediately fell asleep. Twenty minutes later, Panic came onstage, but Mark stayed asleep. I bought my first beer of the season—a can of Bud Light—and listened as Widespread Panic played a song I couldn't identify if offered $10,000. First pitch was five hours away.

I need a real Cubs fan. Someone who has seen Wrigleyville evolve over a few decades. Someone who cares more about the team on the field and less about all this new hoopla in the neighborhood. Someone who would've been watching ESPN at Hi-Tops instead of the stripper on the mechanical horse.

Back in the bleacher line, Andy, a thirty-eight-year-old sign maker, seems to fit the bill. He is wearing jean shorts and a stained yellow T-shirt with short sleeves and no logo. His gut is substantial, his teeth are the same color as his shirt, and his hair is graying. He looks like the type of guy who would have gotten here at 8:30 to stand in line. Turns out that my assumption is right.

"This is the best Opening Day weather I can remember in some time," says Andy, before revealing that he has been to every home opener since 1976. "We're usually freezing by now."

Andy has a long history with the Cubs. When he was younger, his mother would hand him four or five dollars, enough for a bus ride, a ticket to the game, and food. He came of age in the bleachers, about a decade after the original Bleacher Bums made their name in the '60s.

"It's never going back to how it was and you have to accept that," Andy says. "The days of your mother putting you on the train with five bucks is gone. Day-of-game ticket sales are a thing of the past.

"Do I wish it was like it used to be? Sure. You come out here and the place is filled with DePaul and Loyola grads. They're all idiot yuppies and they're not real fans.

"But it works both ways. A full park is not a bad thing. We've got more money to spend on the field. And yeah, a full park adds to the atmosphere, even if not everyone's watching the game."

The Cubs are a huge part of Andy's life. He is completely serious when he claims that the team saved his life in high school.

Back in the '80s, he attended Lane Tech, which is less than two miles from Wrigley on Addison and ranks as the largest high school in the city. When fourth period came around, Andy cut class and hopped the Addison Street bus. Next stop: Wrigley Field.

"My other friends cut class, but they went off and did hard drugs," Andy says. "I headed to Wrigley Field instead. I'm convinced that this place has saved a lot of lives. It sure saved mine."

After graduating, Andy held a number of jobs. He always worked his schedules around Cubs games. In the past, he was offered opportunities to work at the stadium or in bars around the park. He always refused the offers.

"If I worked here, it would ruin it all for me," he says.

"Like how working in the porn industry might ruin sex?"

"I never thought of it that way," Andy says and laughs. "But yeah."

By eleven, the patio is packed at Murphy's Bleachers, the well-known bar located in the shadow of the scoreboard. People are drinking cans of Old Style and Bud Light. The guys in front of us in the line keep leaving to go do Jäger Bombs across the street.

Beer. People. Commotion. It all forms an intrinsic part of the Cubs and the neighborhood in which they reside. It's ironic: Diehard Cubs fans will say there's too much drinking in Wrigleyville, and diehard drinkers will say there's too much emphasis on the Cubs.

I'm here to find where the truth lies. Like any healthy Chicagoan, I like beer and baseball, and not necessarily in that order. As it stands now, I'm standing on the Sheffield wall with a 40-oz. Bud Light in a paper bag.

Mike and Eli say it's all right to be drinking out here, so long as we stay close to the wall and don't wander out into the street.

Nearby, a father stands with his two tiny sons. Pops just paid a scalper $125 apiece for three bleacher tickets, so the excited kids aren't being corrupted by our blatant consumption. Mike and Eli are here with a group of six friends. Each coughed up at least $100 for their seat in the bleachers.

"We don't give a shit what we paid," says Mike. "As long as we're in the game. And we have to be in the bleachers for Opening Day."

They are working-class guys, the same age as me (we graduated high school in '97). A few of them went to community college, a few didn't. They are from Rogers Park, one of the few northern neighborhoods that have been left relatively untouched by gentrification. Nearly all of them manage or work in warehouses.

Andy and I talk about the departure of Sammy Sosa. For thirteen seasons, Sosa served as the Cubs' right fielder, hitting all but 29 of his 574 career home runs while dressed in blue. Three times, he hit over 60 home runs in a season, an unmatched feat. He helped the Cubs to two postseason appearances. While we sat in the bleachers, he charged to his position, tapped his heart, blew kisses, and told us how many outs were in the inning.

But for a number of reasons, Sosa is now persona non grata in Wrigleyville. There was the corked bat incident in '03 and the second-half slump in '04. In the season's final game, the day after the Cubs had been eliminated from postseason contention, Sosa left Wrigley Field while the game was still being played. The team spun the act as the work of a prima donna, allowing the front office to trade Sosa to Baltimore without an outcry from the fans. In March, he appeared before a congressional hearing on steroids and bypassed inquiries by pretending to not understand English.

Most fans are glad that Sosa is gone but Andy and I have mixed emotions. We agree it will be strange to see Jeromy Burnitz, his replacement, run out to Sammy's spot in right field. Sure, it was bad with Sosa at the end, but what about the summer of '98, when he battled with Mark McGwire in the chase to break Roger Maris's record? Are we supposed to completely forget about that?

Eli, having interrupted our conversation, wants to argue the other side.

"Fuck Sammy Sosa," he says between sips of his 40. "All last year, I'd just scream at him, 'You suck, get the hell out of Chicago!' And I swear to God that he'd look at me like he was going to kill me."

Eli is well on his way to being a total mess by the first pitch. Andy has little patience for him.

"Why would you go to the ballpark and not have a good time?" Andy asks. "Why would you go just to be angry?"

"Because I wanted Sammy gone."

A Wrigley Field worker with a name tag that reads "Bill" walks by.

"You can't have open alcohol containers on a public walk-way," he says.

Since my beer has already been finished, he is talking to Mike, Eli, and his friend. They all express mock horror.

"Are you kidding me?" Mike says. "We've been drinking out here for years. No one's ever said anything before."

"Cap 'em up," says Bill.

The guys oblige, but as soon as Bill walks ten feet, they open the bottles again. Eli says not to worry; his father is a Chicago cop who trains police officers. He'll name-drop if there's any more trouble.

No sooner does this come out of Eli's mouth than he and an-other friend are grabbed by a real police officer, not Wrigley Se-curity.

"But my dad's a cop!" says Eli.

"I don't care. Pour it out."

The guys oblige, and after watching the Bud Light trickle down the crumbling curb asphalt and into the street, they leave. It's time for another round of shots at Murphy's. Eli says no, thanks; he's going to smoke a joint before the game instead.

At 11:30, my ticket search goes into high gear. As I mentioned before, I don't have advance tickets to any games this season. I planned it that way. Say what you want about security and peace of mind, some of Wrigley's fun lies in the bob and weave with those asphalt capitalists.

On the surface, the Cubs appear to be a tough ticket. All eighty-one games sold out within a few days in February, marking the second straight season that demand has been high from the start. But I know there's hardly a sporting event where it's impossible to get tickets. Play the waiting game at the Super Bowl and you'll be fine, so long as you don't mind missing the national anthem by Destiny's Child.

And with the Cubs, every moron in the city thinks these tickets are gold. They don't realize that almost forty thousand are available for eighty-one separate dates. They see brokers that are making a lot of money and think they can do the same. But scalpers are making their dough selling the premium seats to law firms and advertising agencies that don't care what they're spending. Meanwhile, regular fans are buying tickets like they're shares of Google stock. Little do they know there isn't much interest in a 500-level seat for a mid-April game against Cincinnati. Advantage: Me.

The ticket story is a little different for Opening Day. The scalpers know they're in a good position and aren't budging early. The regular fan is using most of his tickets—no one's looking to get rid of one here or one there.

With the sun still shining, I walk up Addison, looking for action (or at least the kind involving Cubs tickets). Two girls wearing Cubs ribbons and beads pass by. *Got an extra?* The girls laugh.

"We're just going to the bar," one says. "We're just going to party."

Because I don't have a job anymore, minimizing my ticket expenditures is a priority. The cheaper, the better. I cut over to Clark via Racine. When I reach the Metro, a smallish concert venue on Clark, a scalper offers a ticket. It's 200-level, right behind the plate. Forty bucks.

I offer thirty, which is face, and after a brief haggle, he takes it.

Upon inspection, the ticket looks suspicious. A little worn around the edges. A strange typeface, printed on tickets.com paper.

"You sure this is real?" I ask.

"Aw, come on, man," says the scalper, who is heavyset and wears cornrows. "I don't do that fake shit."

I take his word. And yet when I walk up to the entrance on Clark and Addison, a bit of skepticism still lingers. The ticket taker looks at the ticket and . . . (deep breath) . . . rips it. It's good and my waist clicks through the turnstile.

"Enjoy Opening Day," says the ticket taker.

Finally, baseball. At 1:24 p.m., Kerry Wood delivers the first pitch to Milwaukee's Brady Clark. It's a strike. Baseball at Wrigley Field has begun.

Remember when I wrote the Opening Day weather was great? Well, I was wrong. It is now impossible to be any colder. My seat in section 223 is underneath an overhang, which happens to be the kiss of death. It is an estimated forty-five degrees cooler in the shade. My arms are pulled up inside my fleece, so it looks like I don't have any. Four jacketless women in front of me leave by the start of the second inning.

Wrigley looks great, save for the brown ivy on the walls. It's hard to believe, but the last time I was inside this stadium was for game seven on October 15, 2003. On that day, people stayed in their seats well past the final out that sent the Florida Marlins to the World Series. The fans were shell-shocked as they looked toward the field. Some people couldn't even talk when I approached them. Some looked so distraught that I didn't even try for an interview.

As a reporter, I had to divorce myself from what had just happened. Most people don't believe me, but I didn't feel one way or the other that night. As a journalist, there was a slight feeling of happiness, because it was such a great and dramatic story. If it bleeds, it leads. Looking back, it seems that the ethics of journalism served to break my fall. Maybe deadline adrenaline served as Valium for heartache.

Being able to openly root for the Cubs again feels liberating. But after adhering to the "no cheering in the press box" code, I feel a bit out of place, like a Catholic in a mosque, when it's time to cheer.

Still, that first view of Wrigley, clear after climbing the steps and past the sign featuring a backpedaling, glove-toting cartoon cub (*"Be alert for foul balls!"*), feels religious again. The expanse of the green field seems to represent the season ahead. With only three games behind us, the possibilities seem endless.

This Opening Day marks the last for Wrigley Field as we've known it since 1937. At the end of the season, the Cubs will go ahead with a renovation of the bleachers, adding eighteen hundred seats and presumably changing the feeling of the old ballpark. No one's sure what to expect.

The physical changes will go along with the crowd's altered tenor. Somehow it's palpable that the Cubs are expected to win. Mediocrity will not be laughed away anymore.

Especially not today. The Cubs take a 3–2 lead into the top of the ninth, but closer LaTroy Hawkins surrenders the tying run and the game goes into extra innings. Hawkins receives an avalanche of boos. Milwaukee scores three runs in the top of the twelfth and wins 6–3. The loss drops the Cubs to 1–3, which is definitely not the expected mark out of the gate.

On the way back to the train, I follow three guys wearing Cubs jerseys and carpenter jeans. No one leaving the park, except for the Brewers, is happy. These three guys seem unhappier than most.

"I can't go through this again, man," says one guy. "We should sell our season tickets now, before the bottom falls out."

Chapter Two

The Neighborhood of Baseball

Saturday, April 9—vs. Milwaukee

At noon, four charter buses pull up near the left field gate. A total of approximately three hundred students-drinkers spill out. It's the annual Cubs trip, as staged by the Alphas and Kappas from the University of Illinois. The group has extra tickets and I buy one for $10.

After taking our 200-level seats, it becomes apparent that baseball is secondary to them. Because so many of the Greeks are Chads and Trixies*-in-training, not much else can be expected. The main goal seems to be finding new "activity" partners—presumably for either later tonight or before the next mixer.

In the next row, I notice that one brother has made two new friends in both of his knees. No joke, the kid's head has been buried in his lap since before the first pitch by Carlos Zambrano. His face is not visible to anything but the beer-stained cement, and if there were a responsible parent type around, the kid might be on his way to detox. It is only 1:28.

---

*Derogatory terms used by Chicagoans to describe young and materialistic Lincoln Park residents. Usage: "Did you see how fast that Trixie drove her Jetta away from Starbucks? I bet she's late in picking up Chad from his job at the Board of Trade."

Turns out that Mr. Knees is from my hometown of Bartlett, a suburb located about thirty-five miles northwest of the city. He graduated in 2003, the same year as my sister.

"Hey, we'll see if he knows her," says one of Mr. Knees's friends, the one who dropped the Bartlett knowledge.

"You know what? That's okay," I say.

Common sense would predict that any sudden movement would prove to be a bad decision for Mr. Knees. But common sense left this trip the moment the fraternity lugged thirty cases of Old Style aboard the buses.

"Hey," asks the brother, slapping Mr. Knees on the back. "You know a girl named Kristin?"

Mr. Knees lifts his head, opens his watery eyes, and nods. Seconds later, his cheeks blow outward, as if he's trying to hold a bowl of clam chowder in his mouth.

Then . . . *blaaaaaaak!* The sound of splashing puke is joined by the screams and scrambling of several Illini coeds. Mr. Knees has christened row 17 of section 208 in his own special way.

Unfazed, he heads toward the aisle and staggers toward the exit. No one helps or asks how he's doing. Carlos Zambrano throws a one-hit shutout and the Cubs win 4–0. We do not see Mr. Knees for the rest of the game.

At this point, it is entirely possible that a few readers are headed back to Borders or Barnes & Noble, intending to return this book and give the clerk a mouthful. (*"Two mentions of vomit in the first two chapters!"*) Warranted criticism, but I use this defense as a shield—a reporter cannot dictate what happens around him.

The Mr. Knees story happens to be illustrative *and* informative. If Vegas laid odds on such things, it'd be three to five that Mr. Knees will move to Wrigleyville after his graduation. Indeed, several of his frat brothers said they couldn't wait to move to Chicago so they could see the Cubs whenever they want.

It is that desire that has built up Wrigleyville into the economic force it is today. While any number of factors can be cited for the rise of the neighborhood, I will give most credence to the economic force that is Joe Q. CollegeGrad. Without him, Wrigleyville is still stuck in the 1970s.

As recently as 1980, the neighborhood was far from a baseball paradise. Gang violence and prostitution were prevalent. Drugs were sold on street corners. It grew so bad that when a debate over instituting night games surfaced, people just laughed. The only way to draw people to Wrigley at night would be to give a free bulletproof vest with every hot dog purchase.

Today, it's common to see a single-family home listed for $1.4 million. In the '70s, a million dollars might have bought an entire block.

The gentrification started after Harry Caray left the White Sox in 1982 and moved north to the Wrigley Field broadcast booth. Having pitched Falstaff beer in his earlier days, Caray turned into a "Cub Fan and Bud Man," effectively serving as a larger-than-life advertisement for both baseball and drinking. As this was happening, WGN started invading the nation via homes that were being wired for cable. New fans from Maine to Minnesota watched three-hour commercials for the Cubs, Wrigley Field, and the neighborhood's way of life.

It didn't hurt that the Cubs were good programming. The team won the NL East in 1984 and 1989. Ryne Sandberg and Mark Grace were All-Stars and drew the ladies' interest with their All-American good looks. Andre Dawson became a fan favorite by winning the NL MVP on a last-place team in 1987.

A stream of mostly white college graduates began moving into the brownstones and flats around the park, driving the predominantly Latino population north to Rogers Park and Ravenswood. The developer dollars followed, financing gut rehabs and teardown projects that were replaced by modern buildings with dishwashers and central air. Over the next decade, the commercial properties followed. The prerequisite Starbucks and Irish-themed pubs were erected so the new inhabitants could buy $4.50 caramel macchiatos and $5 pints of Harp.

Blessed for the first time with a steady source of disposable income, the well-educated and white-collar twenty-somethings began turning the North Side into a personal playground. Some were native Chicagoans; others came from around the Midwest. It was easy to identify yourself when meeting a girl in a bar: You were either a Michigan Wolverine, a Purdue Boilermaker, or a Notre Dame Fighting Irish.

The Wrigley Field bleachers and the surrounding bars became sets in the soap opera of their lives. Childhood allegiances to the Tigers or the Indians were forsaken, and the Cubs became the team of choice for many. After leaving school and the excitement of Saturday afternoon football games or Tuesday night basketball, they adopted the Cubs as the new "college" team. The Cubs and Wrigleyville served as more than adequate replacements. Where else could you go to drink beer, watch sports, and flirt with members of the opposite sex?

In time, the Wrigley immigrants in the '80s wrote a universal truth for upwardly-mobile college students from the Midwest. It was a three-pronged agreement, really. You will graduate. You will move to Chicago. You will become a Cubs fan.

On the final day of the opening series, Chicago is still blessed with unseasonably warm weather. Dan calls in the morning and offers a free club box seat. Born in the Detroit suburbs, schooled at the University of Wisconsin (where he served as my college newspaper editor), Dan never paid much attention to the Cubs. Then he moved to Chicago, began working in the mortgage business, and now owns partial season tickets at Wrigley Field. He hasn't been to a Tigers game in over five years.

Dan's seats are in the sun. Score. A common misconception by outsiders is that every seat at Wrigley offers a constant stream of sunbeams. Not so.

It breaks down like this: If you sit in the bleachers, you are guaranteed to bake. Otherwise, it's mostly shade city. The club boxes, lettered by single numbers (1, 2, 3 . . .), usually get a lot of sun during the games. So do some of the field box seats, numbered in the 100s. If you are sitting in the terrace 200s, which is still located on the first level, you are probably screwed. The grandstand provides too much shade. In the 400- and 500-level seats upstairs, the roof provides a cover for almost all of the seats. The bottom line—if you want a seat in the sun, you are going to pay.

Since I'm meeting Dan at the park, I get there early and do a quick lap around the neighborhood. There's another misconception. Wrigleyville is not an actual neighborhood, or at least not one officially recognized by the City of Chicago or the U.S. census takers.

Wrigleyville is part of Lake View, though its exact area is debatable. By my definition, Wrigleyville is anything within four or five blocks of the park. That would set its eclectic boundaries as gritty Irving Park to the north, artsy Belmont to the south, yuppie Southport to the west, and gay Halsted to the east.

The borders for the stadium are easier to discern.

• Left field—Waveland Avenue

Located just north of the left field wall, Waveland is home to several men who target the baseballs that fly out of the park on a regular basis. It's the quietest street of the four, though tour buses congest the street after the game. The famous Budweiser advertisement house, a red sentry that reminds all to drink the King of Beers, is on this street. So is a yellow sixteen-unit building, owned by Cubby Bear and Sports Corner honcho and Wrigleyville real estate baron

George Loukas. He bought the building for $150,000 in 1974. Ladies and gentlemen, this is how you become rich.

• Right field—Sheffield Avenue

Home to popular bars like Murphy's Bleachers, Sports Corner, and Hi-Tops, Sheffield Avenue is one of the best-known border streets. It's not a high-traffic street, but Sheffield happens to be the best place to buy tickets. With a low police presence and the right mix of Everyday Joes and bloodthirsty scalpers, it's hard not to name your price. The rooftop parties dominate Sheffield and before each game, the street is filled with lines of people waiting to climb stairs for one of the best views in baseball. On Sheffield, a rooftop sign reads, *"Eamus Catuli,"* Latin for Let's go, Cubs.

• First base line—Addison Street

Perhaps the least utilitarian of the streets, Addison features the famous El stop and the Taco Bell, but little else. There's a lot of bus traffic and an abundance of pushy and rude scalpers, plus little sidewalk space on the Wrigley side of the street. Addison, however, gets bonus points for being a man-made tributary to Lake Michigan. Walk ten blocks east and you'll end up wet.

• Third base line—Clark Street

Because it runs on a diagonal, Clark is the only road not on a parallel path with the walls of Wrigley. Doesn't matter. Clark runs all the way downtown, and the path is paved with bars and restaurants. Head south on Clark from Irving Park Road and you will hit Ginger Man Tavern, Metro, Smart Bar, Full Shilling, Trace, Raw, Yak-zies,

Bernie's, Casey Moran's, Cubby Bear, Vines, Bar Louie, Goose Island, Mullen's, Sluggers, the Wild Hare, John Barleycorn, Moe's Cantina, Irish Oak, Merkle's, and Red Ivy on Clark. That's twenty-one bars in a stretch of less than a quarter mile: a Murderer's Row for the thirsty people of Chicago.

Dan's seats are just past third base, nine rows from the field and in the middle of a staggering number of good-looking women. In particular, there is a tall blonde, probably in her mid-thirties, sitting in front of us. Dan bites into a chicken sandwich while I chomp on a pretzel. When we are not exchanging snippets of baseball wisdom, talking about poker, or watching the Cubs mount their comeback against the Brewers, we are staring at this woman.

In the middle of the fourth, the blonde stands up, pulls her Cubs sweatshirt over her head and takes it off. Underneath is a Cubs halter top that shows off her white skin, the unfortunate victim of a Midwestern winter. She is still stunning. After scoring her as the Ceremonial First Babe, I notice that we are far from the girl's only fans. I catch another guy looking over; he responds with a thumbs-up.

Dan explains that he had a part in the disrobing.

"In my head, I just kept saying, 'Take off the sweatshirt, take off the sweatshirt.' And then she did it!" Dan says. "Do you see what a positive mental attitude can do?"

Oh, the beautiful women of Chicago. How I missed you. For one, there are a greater number of women as compared to Kansas City, which happened to be Leavenworth prison for single guys. It's not that there weren't any good-looking girls there, especially if you like blondes (and let's hope you do). It's just that all of them happened to be married/engaged/betrothed/in a serious relationship by the age of twenty. A typical introduction: *"Kevin, I'd like for you to meet my husband, Darren. Can you believe I met my soul mate in Emporia? I mean, what are the odds?"*

In Chicago, we are part of a much larger dating pool. According to the 2000 census, Lake View had 94,817 people, forming the second-largest neighborhood in the city. Of that number, 47,516 were women, compared to 47,301 men. While that's not quite the ratio that Jan and Dean might have required, I'll take it. The numbers are on my side—and that's even before you throw in my dashing good looks, unparalleled wit, and complete lack of employment.

Because heading to Wrigley Field is perhaps the most popular summer activity in Chicago, it's likely that I'll leer and/or ogle every twenty-something girl on the North Side this spring and summer. So be it. We all have our crosses to bear.

Heading into the bottom of the twelfth inning, the Cubs and Brewers are tied at five. Shortstop Nomar Garciaparra is not having the best of days. He is 0 for 5 and has failed to deliver in two late-inning situations. He is batting .143.

Since he came to the Cubs from Boston last July, we have tried hard to like him. He reminds us of ourselves. We rise to our feet, yelling ourselves hoarse in hopes that Nomar will produce a quintessential Cubs moment, one worthy of a scrapbook. It has yet to come. With every pop-up or strikeout, the frustration is tangible, both from Garciaparra and the fans.

We feel fortunate that he is here. Cubs fans' loyalty at the turnstiles has been rewarded with contracts for guys like Garciaparra, Mark Prior, Greg Maddux, Derrek Lee, and Aramis Ramirez. These are bona fide superstars, and gone are the days when off-season acquisitions like George Bell and Dave Patterson sparked false hope. At least we're coming to games with a loaded gun and not Steve Buechele at third.

Instead of Garciaparra, another new addition, right fielder Jeromy Burnitz, leads off the bottom of the twelfth with a triple. Minutes later, Todd Hollandsworth hits a chopper up the middle, sending Burnitz home for a win that brings the Cubs' record to 3–3. It took four hours, but the year's first home series is officially in the books.

Chapter Three

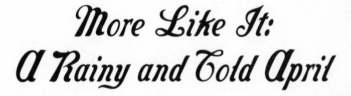

More Like It:
A Rainy and Cold April

April 11-13—vs. San Diego

Time for a quick lesson on the history of Lake View. The neighborhood was first established when Joseph Sheffield, a cotton exporter from Alabama, could not resist the urge to become a fast-talking, marijuana-growing street hustler. So, in the 1850s, Sheffield headed north to Chicago and started a nursery.*

After a few years, Sheffield's business took off. He founded the Chicago, Rock Island, and Pacific Railroad and started developing an area to the north of Chicago, later known as the town of Lake View.

After acquiring land adjacent to Clark Street, Sheffield went about naming the new roads. One street was easy—he named it Sheffield. But when it came time to name the intersecting road, he found it was flooded from Lake Michigan. Sheffield named the road Waveland.

Lake View drew a large number of German immigrants and those who wanted a bucolic escape from the choking congestion

---

*Completely true, except for the part about pot, which was added because, let's face it, there is nothing really exciting about a cotton exporter moving to Chicago to start a nursery.

of the burgeoning city. It was a little like the Hamptons, minus Paris Hilton and with a lot more horse-drawn carts. When the Great Fire ravaged Chicago in 1871, many Chicagoans headed north. Lake View was one of the few areas to boast houses and factories made of stone. In time, the neighborhood became more focused on industry, and was annexed by Chicago in 1889.

Fifteen years earlier, a Lutheran minister named William Passavant had come into several acres filled with cottonwoods and ash trees. Passavant built St. Mark's Lutheran Church and, in 1891, opened the Theological Seminary of the Evangelical Lutheran Church. He had six students.

By 1910, the seminary had grown tired of the growing industrialism in the neighborhood. The seminary moved west and sold the land to an investor from Milwaukee, who hoped to lease the land to railroads. When that didn't work, the land was sold to Charles Weeghman, a part owner of the Whales, a Federal League baseball team. In 1914, Weeghman Park opened, built at a cost of what Alex Rodriguez makes in roughly two games (or $250,000).

In 1916, the Cubs (with Weeghman as their new owner) played their first game on the grounds. Someone brought a bear cub, which always seems strange. Take a look at old sporting event footage. This may be a generalization, but doesn't it seem that there were an extraordinary number of live animals at pre–World War II sporting events? People did amazing things for entertainment before cable television. And if there was a more entertaining mix than dangerous animals and large and noisy crowds, they apparently didn't know about it.

As I walk to the game against San Diego on a cold Monday morning, I ponder Wrigley's previous incarnations. That a seminary was once located on the grounds of what would become Wrigley Field is always cited as more than appropriate. Or perhaps not, considering there isn't a sporting venue in America where more prayers have gone unanswered. The Cubs haven't won a title since 1908.

1908.

On a line by itself, it looks pathetic. It seems even more dismal if it bounces around the brain for a few minutes.

1908!

Oh, damn it all to hell.

Since the Cubs last won a World Series, America has endured eighteen presidents, nine popes, and six wars. While the Scopes Monkey Trial and Teapot Dome Scandal sound ancient (and they are), both took place after the '08 title. Other unlikely events have occurred: the sinking of the unsinkable *Titanic*, the United States landing a man on the moon, two visits from Halley's comet, and the ability to distribute doctored nudes of Christina Aguilera in milliseconds over the Internet.

Lee Iacocca once said the secret in life was to "not die while waiting for success," but many Cubs fans have had little choice in the matter. We can only live for so long.

There are times when the ninety-seven-year drought depresses me and I wonder if that championship day will ever come. Then there's the White Sox (and we'll get to them later), who have the next longest drought, dating back to 1917. What have we done in Chicago to deserve this? How can such an international city with virtually limitless resources go 185 combined years without rewarding their fans with a title at the end? How can we be classified as a losing city? That title should be for places like Pittsburgh and Houston and Milwaukee. But definitely not Chicago.

That we care so much is a wonder. The question has been asked before, but why do the collective fortunes of a team owned by a conglomerate like the Tribune Company matter? Most of us have never met the twenty-five men who make up the Cubs roster. Most of our career incomes will never come close to matching what a mediocre shortstop makes in one year.

So why do we care what happens to them?

The answer lies not in "rooting for laundry," as Jerry Seinfeld once said, but in the epic chase that the Cubs' ineptitude has created. Perhaps the recently liberated Red Sox fans can attest to this—a World Series title seems like a cure-all elixir for endless years of waiting and wishing. Maybe a ticker-tape parade could make us feel better. We just want to see how this play is supposed to end. We want our money's worth.

There is a stereotype that Cubs fans don't mind losing, so the national media paints us as the forgetful and lovable drunks of the sporting world. While the scenes of packed bars certainly don't help, I don't know one true Cubs fan who enjoys being on the losing end. It's not cute or admirable. Maybe there is a bit of a "har, har, boy do we suck" in our bellyaching, but that's just a defense mechanism. Outsiders can't laugh at us if we're the ones telling the joke.

Seven games into the season and it has become apparent that the mood in Wrigleyville will be changing daily. The Cubs fell to San Diego 1–0 on Monday, thanks in part to a dropped fly by Jeromy Burnitz and general impotence from the offense.

Today, Wednesday, April 13, will be different. After a rainout on Tuesday, the Cubs and Padres will play a doubleheader. One price, two games. Mark Prior, one of the top pitchers in the National League and a franchise cornerstone, will make his first start of the season in the second game. I have two tickets for the bleachers and it's nice out. When I think about why I left my job, it was based on the *idea* of a day like this.

After packing a lunch and a bag of peanuts, I head to Wrigley, scalp another bleacher seat, and then leave two tickets at will call for Haydn and Joe, friends who are joining me for the day.

It's been three years since I've been in the bleachers. But as I climb the spiraling ramp toward right field, it feels familiar. In high school, we didn't consider sitting anywhere else in the stadium. It was different back then; seats were only six bucks if you came on the right day, twelve dollars for regular games. Things have changed in eight years. Today's bleacher ticket, which is priced as one of only six "value" games, is $15.

Thirty-five "regular" games will cost $28 each in the bleachers, while the remaining forty games are classified as "prime" dates. (These games include every contest against the White Sox, Red Sox, and Cardinals, plus all but one home game in July and August.) These tickets are a shake-your-head $38.

The worst part is that bleacher tickets aren't even available on the day of the game. The Cubs used to hold a certain number to be sold before the gates opened. *No mas.* Now the only option for latecomers is to buy a bleacher seat from a scalper. For the in-demand games, the prices are ridiculous—$75 and up. Every scalper claims to have "bleachers for sale," but if you buy from the guys down on Addison, caveat emptor. Often their "bleacher" is really just a standing-room-only.

Anyone who has sat in the bleachers more than once has his or her favorite spot. Mine happens to be in right field, all the way at the end of the section, three rows from the field.

For one, the right fielder stands no more than twenty feet away, making for easy access to both praise and clever heckles. When Sammy was here, he carried a small whistle that was attached to his glove. Between outs, you could yell, "Sammy, blow your whistle!" and he'd do it. That one was a crowd-pleaser.

On the flip side, opposing players can hear every shout, scream, and Oedipus-related joke directed their way. It's a lot like watching a lion at the zoo. Sometimes you yell and the lion looks at you. Sometimes he just yawns and looks the other way. When you throw in the wire basket on the outfield wall, it's not hard to imagine Burnitz as a specimen in captivity.

The other best thing about my seat is the view. It's close enough to track the path of the pitch, and most of the people down here are actually interested in watching the game. That's an uncommon luxury in the bleachers, where so many come to tan and socialize. If you're in row five or higher, forget about it— you're more likely to hear about someone's portfolio than the reasons for Sosa's ouster from the team.

In the fourth inning of game one, with the Cubs already down 5–0, center fielder Corey Patterson comes to the plate. Padres right-hander Jake Peavy delivers a pitch and Patterson connects. From our viewpoint, it's a curving line drive. After it straightens out from its early bend, we see that it's heading directly toward us.

The wait between Patterson's blast and the subsequent touchdown is both exhilarating and terrifying. Right now, it feels like we've just tossed a beer at Ron Artest and are waiting to be blindsided by a Stephen Jackson haymaker. The three (maybe four?) seconds seems longer than it should be. I use this time to assess my gloveless options, and then ask myself two questions:

(1) *Am I willing to break my hand for a baseball? (Or in the more likely case of a misjudged fly, my nose?)*

And—

(2) *What are the potential social ramifications of using a girl as a human shield in this situation? That would definitely make* Sports Center, *right? Laughingstock status, no?*

As a male Kaduk, I have no choice but to make a play. In 1984, my father set a standard of manhood that neither my brother nor I have been able to match. Before the start of a White Sox–Mariners tilt at Comiskey Park, the old fam was watching a little batting practice. My brother and I stood in the front row, clutching mitts (like we could have caught anything) above our heads. Mom, five months pregnant with my sister, sat a few rows back.

Minutes later, Seattle's Gorman Thomas let forth with an epic drive that, as my parents tell it, was heading straight for my mother's belly, with Kristin inside it. Only a quick leap and hand deflection by Dad saved the two females in our family. Dad was left with a busted-up, purple-and-blue hand (we stayed for the game though), and we were left with a Stormin' Gorman baseball.

It remains a family heirloom.

San Diego right fielder Brian Giles looks up, but no one in the bleachers notices. Our mob is about to make the play. Judging by the trajectory, I've definitely got a shot at corralling my first game ball. I've been to hundreds of games and this is my first shot at a game-worn memento.

The ball is five feet away. Fifteen people squeeze within a five-foot radius. With outstretched arms, the crowd looks like a hurricane-bent tree—except all the diagonal-leaning branches are made of skin and bones. I am in the middle of the maelstrom. The ball is headed straight at me.

It's going to hit my hand. Maybe there will be a fracture. Definitely a lot of bruises. Just like Dad. But can I get my hands around it and fight off the herd?

I don't even get the chance. At the last possible second, a large man wearing a tie-dyed T-shirt throws his hands in the path of the Rawlings.

Smack! Everyone instinctively starts looking toward the ground. Tie Dye didn't catch the ball clean and it's down there, rolling around in the beer puddles and peanut droppings. We are busy looking in the first two rows. Everyone from the first two rows is looking back at us. It's a mad scramble, all for a ball from a woefully underachieving center fielder.

Finally, I look toward my feet. The ball, with its red seams and blue printing, is resting up against my size-thirteen Puma. It's too late, though. Danny from Park Ridge (the guy sitting next to me) bends over and gets a hand on it. At the same time, a teenager in the first row, wearing a backward Cubs hat, puts a hand in the scrum. A second later, he's holding it above his head, prizing it like a grizzly bear with an upstream salmon.

The rest of the swarm launches into the obligatory post-ball action. *Holy shit? Did you see that we were that close?* (Shake head, sit down, put palms on both knees, shake head again, hold up hands to estimate distance to ball, catch breath.) *We were that close!*

"Damn, I could have had it," I say.

The big guy in the tie-dyed shirt, who is favoring his right hand, scoffs.

"Ah, it's just a baseball," he says. "You get it here. You take it home. You put it on a shelf and then forget about it. It's not that big of a deal."

Strange how priorities can change. Thirty seconds ago, corralling "just a baseball" was his sole purpose in life.

I happened to be lying when I claimed the mood in Wrigleyville was changing day by day. Now it's hour by hour. The Cubs lose the first game to San Diego 8–3, no thanks to Kerry Wood's poor effort. It leaves us asking if Wood's twenty-strikeout game in 1998 ever really happened. Game two now seems like the first must-win of the season. (And yes, it's silly to call the ninth game of the season a "must-win" . . . but how else to describe the high expectations in Chicago this year?)

Mark Prior saves the day. Making his first start after missing most of spring training with an injury, Prior pitches six shutout innings in an 8–3 victory. By the end of the second inning, the Cubs lead 7–0, making it safe to socialize with fellow bleacherites.

Before long, we are talking with the tie-dyed shirt guy (Aaron, a real estate guru) and his friend (Matt, a salesman). They are in their mid-thirties, have fading hairlines, and are downing beers. It being Wednesday, I ask if they went to work before the game.

"Define 'working,'" Aaron says. "My cell phone is on. That's the extent of how much I'm working today."

Matt and I end up conversing a bit more. He notices my University of Wisconsin T-shirt and notes that he's a fellow Badger. His dog is named Mifflin, a nod to the famous off-campus block-party street in Madison.

Matt, or "Soks"—I have been instructed to call him by an abbreviation of his last name—is recently divorced.

"What are you doing for the next homestand?" Soks asks. "I've got some tickets. It's going to be a big party. We're celebrating my return to drinking."

And how long have you been sober?

Two years?

Three?

"Three weeks," Soks replies. "I take off three weeks from drinking every year. I stop on the night of the [NCAA national] championship game and start again in late April."

Soks is my kind of guy. We exchange numbers and promise to call each other. And while that seems weird, I promise it wasn't.

Chapter Four

*On Rainouts and
Slow Starts*

April 22–24—vs. Pittsburgh

"**D**id you hear what happened to Ronnie?"

It's the top question around Wrigleyville as the Pirates come in for a three-game weekend set. If you know about the Cubs, you know about Ronnie.

At sixty-three, Ronnie "Woo-Woo" Wickers has been coming out to Wrigley for as long as anyone can remember. He's an African-American gentleman with a halting walk and a high-pitched but piercing shout of encouragement—"Cubs! *Woo!* World! *Woo!* Series! *Woo!*" The cry has become so ubiquitous that many people believe Woo is his real last name.

"*Hey, do you know Ronnie Wickers?*"

"*No.*"

"*Well, how about Ronnie?*"

"*Oh, you mean Ronnie Woo-Woo? Of course!*"

Since he wears a full Cubs uniform—both in season and out—Ronnie is easy to identify. On Opening Day, I saw him walking east on Addison, a cute girl on each arm. He's forever obliging photo requests, signing autographs, and issuing fist pounds to anyone who asks. On off days, he makes money by washing the windows of Wrigleyville businesses. Go to a Subway and order a sandwich, there's Ronnie, squeegeeing away.

Over the years, his story has become well known, and Wickers himself was the feature of a documentary named *Woo Life* released earlier this season. Abused by his father and raised by his grandmother, Wickers turned to the Cubs for salvation in the 1950s. He's had some rough times over the years, battling homelessness and substance abuse, but the Cubs have been a constant. In 1987, he took a day job delivering pizzas, causing him to miss most home games. A rumor started: Ronnie Woo had been murdered.

But eighteen years later, he's still here, bouncing around Wrigleyville like a bumper car. He's a serial cameo artist, a Great Wanderer forever entering the scene of a thousand Wrigley movies and always stealing the scene. For some (okay, most), Ronnie and his wooing are nothing more than an annoyance. (One of my favorite Woo-Woo memories includes Ronnie standing outside an arriving Atlanta Braves bus and being told, point-blank, to "shut the fuck up" by a pitching coach.)

For others, a day without a Ronnie appearance is an incomplete trip to the ballpark.

"Did you hear what happened to Ronnie?"

Seems that Ronnie's season, like that of his favorite team, is off to a less than auspicious start. On April 18, Ronnie was walking near Clark and Addison when a Ford Taurus backed into him, sending Ronnie to the ground. The damages were minimal—a hospital visit revealed a headache and a sore elbow—but still enough to warrant a mention in the city's newspapers.

Noon on Friday. It is raining.

This is problematic because whenever there is a rain delay, TV stations tend to play "Here Comes That Rainy Day Feeling Again"

by the Fortunes. And then—and you can put money on this—
they follow with shots of the rain-pummeled tarp, huddled fans
in the grandstand, and bored middle relievers in the dugout.
That's all well and good, but the Fortunes have a way of burrow-
ing into your mind and not leaving. In fact, there are few songs
tougher to erase.

I'm whistling it while dropping down the stairs at the Addison
Street station. The Cubs are back after a seven-day trip to Pittsburgh, Cincinnati, and St. Louis, but it's doubtful they'll play the
Pirates today. A check of the Doppler shows nothing but green
(green!) all the way to Nebraska. People are furiously trying to
dump their tickets, which is stupid because a rainout will give
them a full refund or tickets to the makeup.

I can't take advantage of the eager sellers. Soks (pronounced
"soaks") called earlier this morning, leaving instructions to meet
up at the Full Shilling on Clark. "I've got a ticket for you," went
the message. "Plus the Shilling gives you a free hot dog for every
beer you buy, so we've got lunch covered."

Soks is clearly a genius. At least by Wrigleyville standards. I
dash through the rain and head toward the northern part of
Clark, toward the Shilling. It's not a bad bar. Yes, it's got the Irish-
theme-in-a-box thing going (i.e., all the "genuine" shillelagh
decorations probably come from a warehouse in Phoenix). But
it's cozy and the lighting gives it a slight hint of character. The
flat-screen TVs look good. So does the waitstaff.

The bar also has a game-day "special"—$3 domestic drafts. In
theory, this is fantastic. In practice, the deal involves a midriff-
baring bartender pushing a tiny and flimsy Solo cup of lukewarm
Lite your way.

Len Kasper and Bob Brenly are currently on the flat-screen
above the bar. The tarp-covered field is in the background. *"We're
going to try to wait this one out,"* they say.

"What the hell does Bob Brenly know about Chicago?"

The question comes from a man to my left. A green bottle of Heineken and a shot of Jäger rest at the tips of his hands. He needs an answer.

The query is not a bad one. Kasper and Brenly are in their third week as the Cubs' television broadcast team, and the early reviews have been less than stellar. Kasper, who formerly did play-by-play for the Marlins and Brewers, fits the role of every youngish broadcaster. Smart, clean-cut, and methodical, Kasper reminds you of the successful next-door neighbor, the one who somehow stays likeable despite the Beemer in the drive. At the same time, he's not going to surprise you or reveal much character. Also, Kasper has a tendency to sound like Kermit the Frog, and a despicable résumé line (at least to Chicagoans): He once played a role on Packers' halftime shows.

Brenly's presence, meanwhile, is a real head-scratcher. After serving three and a half years as Arizona's manager (which included the 2001 World Series championship), Brenly landed in the spot vacated by Steve Stone, the exalted color man who was chased away last season by the public gripes of Dusty Baker, Moises Alou, and Kent Mercker. Brenly has no ties to Chicago— didn't grow up here, didn't play here, didn't manage here. He worked with Harry Caray and the Cubs for two seasons in the early '90s, but that seems beside the point. Brenly has this weird mustache, and it makes me think of the best T-shirt I've ever seen: *Guns don't kill people. People with mustaches kill people.* Don't get me wrong. Brenly seems like a nice enough guy. It's just that he's less than inspiring when his mouth is opened.

"What the hell does Bob Brenly know about Chicago?"

The question rattles. At its base lies an essential truth about those from the Windy City. We can be inclusive at the same time we're being exclusive. The question reflects our view; we certainly don't want non-Chicagoans coming in and talking about *our* Cubs. At the same time, this man has started up a conversation with me, a total stranger, in a bar. He just assumed I was a Chicagoan. *One of us.* I could have been from Tacoma or La Jolla or Trenton.

Here's the thing about Chicagoans. We need to be around you for a bit, need to sniff you out, find out if you're trustworthy, *a good guy to be around.* Once you're in, you're part of the club. One of the guys. A Chicagoan. No one remembers that Harry Caray was from St. Louis or Jack Brickhouse from Peoria.

Ron Santo is from the state of Washington. So is Ryne Sandberg. Mike Ditka, the ultimate Chicago icon, came from Pennsylvania. Brian Urlacher is a New Mexican. All these guys turned out to be more than just fine with us.

Because I have no idea what Brenly knows about Chicago, I circumvent the man's question by offering a summary of the argument above. In turn, I ask him why he thinks Chicagoans might be tentative in letting an "outsider" in the broadcast booth.

"I don't know," says the man, whose name turns out to be Mark. "I think we want people who are really going to feel our pain if we lose . . . or really go nuts if we win. Why do you think we liked Harry Caray so much?

"You see Brenly up there and he's wearing his World Series ring from Arizona and it's like he doesn't have anything invested but a contract in this whole deal. We either want you in all the way or we don't want you at all."

With the rain still pouring, I continue my conversation with Mark. Two more rounds of Lite pass, as do two more updates by Kasper and Brenly. It doesn't look good. The Shilling, which was near empty when I arrived, is slowly filling with fans who took detours from the turnstiles. (Once you're in at Wrigley, you're in.) Still no sign of Soks. He's not picking up his cell phone.

Mark grew up in the suburbs before heading to Southern Illinois to pursue mechanical engineering. Now he owns a machine shop at Addison and Pulaski, plus Cubs season tickets, terrace box, third base side.

We order another round. I open my notebook and let Mark sound off. For ten minutes, I do nothing but write and nod.

"I was so sick of dealing with people today, so I decided to come down here," Mark says. "Even though it was raining when I left, I just needed to get away. I told everyone at work, don't call unless it's an extreme emergency. Friday games are my type of reward for a long week at work.

"Last year was the best Cubs team I've ever seen. I'm thirty-five years old and we've never had a better chance to get to the World Series. But then the injuries came and the players started whining. People are so angry at Dusty Baker, but what about Sammy Sosa and Moises Alou? What about LaTroy Hawkins? I've always said that Cubs managers are forgiven and then forgotten. It'll work the same way when Dusty leaves town.

"The Cubs find so many original ways to lose. It's just stupid. But then you've got all these people now that are trying to blame it on the 'Curse of the Billy Goat?' You've got to be kidding me. How about the fact that we've just never been a very good team?

"I've been coming out to Wrigley since I was a kid. I'll probably never stop coming. That's just the Chicago way. We support our teams. We're the third-biggest city in the country and we don't get the love that New York or Los Angeles gets. So we turn to our sports teams. We watch the Cubs and Sox during the summer, then the Bears and Bulls during the winter. Yeah, they always disappoint us, but we're not going to go anywhere."

Kasper and Brenly come on one more time. Game canceled. Makeup date: Thursday, July 14. Mark and I sit back and shake our heads. Still, it's fun to sit inside here, at 2:41 p.m., with everyone else at work while the cold rain creates a dreary April day.

"Some people may say this was a waste of time," Mark says. "But I don't think so. No day at Wrigley is ever a waste."

Soks calls the next morning.

"Dude, rough night on Thursday," he says. "I started off for Wrigley, but had to turn back and go to bed. Sorry, man. We'll get 'em next time, bro."

April 25–27—vs. Cincinnati

So much for expectations. Because these are the Cubs and not the Yankees, we find ourselves already on the ropes. It started that opening weekend at home when second baseman Todd Walker injured his left knee in the extra innings of the Sunday victory over Milwaukee. It continued when shortstop Nomar Garcia-parra, the walking *Sports Illustrated* cover jinx, suffered a groin injury in a 3–1 win over St. Louis on April 20. Walker's going to miss at least a month. Nomar's out until August.

All this on top of Saturday's game, a freezing and windy affair that saw LaTroy Hawkins blow his second save of the season with two earned runs in the Cubs' 4–3 loss. A 5–2 victory on Sunday brought the team to an even 9–9 record, but something already doesn't feel right. *Danger, Dusty Baker!*

There's one positive in the team's relatively slow start. The buyers hold the power position in the early ticket market. Tickets are starting at face value and dropping from there. Like I said before, the market is flooded. Mix a slow start with cold weather and you've got more people deciding to stay home and watch all eighty-four hours of the NFL Draft.

On Saturday, I bought a $40 ticket behind home plate for $15. On Sunday, a little bit of waiting produced a desperate situation for those walking around with bricks of tickets.

When dealing with the secondary ticket market, it's important to act like getting into the game is of minimal importance. In fact, sometimes it's better to act like you're on your way to do something else. Go to the Cubs game? Well, I *guess* I could. . . .

"But all I've got is three dollars," I said on Sunday, pulling three Washingtons from my sweatshirt. This is an old trick. You wouldn't taunt a pit bull with a porterhouse, and along similar lines, you should never flash a wad of twenties to a scalper.

"That's fine," said the scalper, quickly pressing the ticket in my hand at almost a 90 percent discount.

They say you gotta get while the getting is good, and that certainly applies here. It's going to be warm in a few weeks and better teams will be coming to town, and the scalpers won't be nearly as agreeable to lower prices. For now, I'll take what I want, triumphant in my haggling skills. The good scalpers realize they can't win all the time.

My brother, Dave, three years my junior, meets me at the Belmont stop. We are an interesting study in fraternal contrast, but I suspect we aren't that much different from other sets of siblings.

When we were younger, Dave dutifully filled the role of younger brother. When I needed a right fielder, a roller hockey goalie or H-O-R-S-E opponent, Dave was my guy. Over time he became a serviceable Little League third baseman, an aficionado of the San Francisco 49ers, and an efficient groundskeeper for our backyard Wiffle ball field. I was better at basketball; he was superior with a pair of skates and a stick. We were probably equal on the baseball diamond. That is to say both of our careers ended when pitchers started throwing curves. (Somehow our younger sister, Kristin, a varsity soccer player, became a much better athlete than either of us ever was.)

Despite his talents, Dave always realized sports were my territory. I knew all the coaches, players, and requisite stats. When it became clear he would never eclipse my knowledge, he turned to another field. At thirteen, he began buying guitars, grew his hair long, and hung posters of Kurt Cobain on his wall. Music would be his area of expertise.

And so he went, mastering both the guitar and bass while forming a band, Five to Fade, which now plays gigs in the Lincoln Park bars. During the day he's a sound engineer, lording it over the mixing board for Chicago's biggest advertising firms. At twenty-three, he has his shit together.

We head north up Clark, stopping at Jimmy John's for sandwiches that we can take into the game. Dave is wearing a backward Cubs hat with a messenger's bag hung over his shoulder. I wouldn't say that Dave is a fair-weather fan, but he has definitely ratcheted his interest up since the 2003 season. Now he watches the Internet GameCasts at work, follows the action in the newspapers, and sends me instant messages that say things like, "Boy, the Cubs really sucked today, didn't they?"

Dave is able to attend today's game because it is the first of twenty-four night games scheduled for this season. For the occasion I have purchased two bleacher tickets on eBay from a man in Naperville. Five bucks under face.

We take my regular spot in the third row of right field. For some reason, no matter how late you show up, the seats are always open. Dave leaves and comes back five minutes later with two paper cups full of Old Style.

"Dude, they've got corn dogs at the concession stand!" he reports.

Dave starts yelling at Cincinnati right fielder Austin Kearns, and for the first time since I moved home, it hits me that I missed being able to call him up and say, "Wanna go see the Cubs tonight?"

Michael Benson, the author of *Ballparks of North America*, has the first and last word on night games on the North Side: "The first time you see Wrigley at night, it feels like you just saw your second grade teacher at the supermarket."

Benson is right. Almost seventeen years after the first night game at Wrigley, something still doesn't feel right. I've been to a whopping total of four Cubs night games since 1988. Adding a large number of games to that total doesn't seem very appealing.

Night baseball is for places like Philadelphia or New York. It definitely still doesn't belong at Clark and Addison. Before this season, the team was limited to eighteen night games per season. This year the limit has been raised to twenty-four games. In a few more seasons, the number will reach thirty.

Unacceptable, say some residents of Wrigleyville, who detest what night games bring—namely, forty thousand strangers hell-bent on making noise, drinking beer, and, as is so often cited by these residents, pissing on front lawns and by alleyway Dumpsters. But with their protests ultimately falling in the path of the Tribune Company's intense drive for increased profits, there is little that can be done.

Wrigley Field played host to more than seventy years of exclusive day baseball, and for that we have Adolf Hitler and the nation of Japan to thank. At the end of the 1941 season, plans were made to install lights for the beginning of the next. Then came Pearl Harbor, and the United States entered World War II. The material for the light standards was donated to the war effort. In later years, as every other stadium went with lights, Cubs owner P. K. Wrigley realized he was marketing something no other team had—the "ability" to play each game during the day. And so went the Cubs until 1988, when the draw of increased after-work crowds ultimately proved to be too much for the Tribune Company (which bought the team from the Wrigley family in 1981).

Night games at Wrigley are a different beast altogether. While a daytime crowd definitely does its share of drinking, the attitude at night seems to be "because there is a cover of darkness, we can get away with more." And so, over the years, Cubs fans have marked night games by throwing trash on the field, stealing the hat off the head of Dodger catcher Chad Kreuter in a famous incident in 2000, and generally being a bit more rambunctious than usual.

In this game alone (which the Cubs will take by a score of 10–6 over Cincinnati), we rise thirteen times so that the guy sitting next to us can go buy beer. During the seventh inning, I ask him who's winning. "Not sure," says the guy, grinning with the proud ignorance only a drunk could muster.

Over the next two days, the Cubs finish their series with Cincinnati. I skip Tuesday's game (my first no-show of the season) when an offer of 25¢ chicken wings and $4.00 pitchers at Kincade's in Lincoln Park proves too enticing. "Besides, the game will be on television," goes the rationalization in my head. The field trip is a profitable one, and not just for the grub. We meet Sue Ellen five pitchers in, after the Cubs' pitching has been pasted 11–9. She is plastered and about to fish off the company pier with a coworker. Still, she takes the time to talk to us and lets us in on a secret. During the next homestand, her company will be hosting a Sheffield rooftop party for its clients. If we want, she can sneak us on the list. We'll have to pretend we're representing a company, but it shouldn't be much of a problem.

"Do you guys want to go up there?" Sue Ellen asks.

"Putusonthelist," we say simultaneously.

Done, says Sue Ellen, before returning to her workplace paramour.

"How do we know this girl?" I whisper to my friend Brian.

"Remember Marc from UW?" he asks. "She used to sleep with him."

"Fair enough," I say and order another round of drinks.

* * *

On Wednesday, I arrive at Wrigley two hours early, scalp a bleacher for $10, and head to right field for batting practice. I sit in the last row, hoping to pick off any blasts that fail to clear the fence onto Sheffield. Five minutes later, Ken Griffey Jr. steps into the cage. The area around me is clear. There's a smattering of people throughout the bleachers. Wednesday can be a tough day to draw a crowd. (The game is still sold out.)

And then it comes.

A long sky-driven ball that is easily tracked against the gray April afternoon sky. The ball glides over everyone, hits the chain-link fence, and rebounds right back into . . . my gut. My arms instinctively fold around it. The pursuing crowd gapes at me. I look down at the ball—small and white.

Mine.

It doesn't beat a hand bruiser from Gorman Thomas, but it's from a future Hall of Famer. That has to count for something.

I sit by myself, hunched like a widower in a church pew, cracking peanuts and listening to Pat Hughes and Ron Santo call the game on a $5 transistor from Wal-Mart. The Cubs fall down early and enter the bottom of the seventh trailing 7–4. But first baseman Derrek Lee, who has already homered once, ties the game with a three-run dinger to left. He now has twenty-seven RBIs in April, the most in the majors.

In the ninth inning (after an improbable 1-2-3 inning from LaTroy Hawkins), Corey Patterson comes to the plate. Facing Cincinnati reliever Matt Belisle, Patterson lifts a pitch that rises toward right center. . . . It rises, rises until falling into a pit of a dozen reaching hands in the bleachers. The weekday crowd yells its approval as Patterson gets mobbed by teammates at home plate, and then, thirty seconds later, we are heading down the spiral ramp toward the bleachers exit. We are a moving mob, happy and content as the Cubs prepare for a trip to Houston.

Frequently Asked Questions

May

Q: *How's the new place?*
A: The biggest change I've noticed is that I again have to pay rent with American currency. This kind of sucks because Jedd and Brian, my gracious hosts for the past month, were happy whenever I put a new case of Miller Lite in their fridge.

Q: *OK, but how's the place?*
A: Great. It's close to about 152 different bars, and we've already hit about 75 percent of them. Last night we tried to enter one bar, but Groves started swearing and talking about whiskey when the bouncer asked for his ID. "Sir, you've been overserved," Groves was told. So we went to Wrigleysville Dogs and Art bought everyone a corn dog. Then I walked home two blocks and drunk-dialed every female in my cell phone until someone picked up. It was 2:21 in the morning when Jen finally answered.

Q: *Are you going to keep talking about alcohol? Or are you going to tell me about your new apartment?*
A: Right . . . but it's just that booze is so prevalent in Wrigleyville. Almost as prevalent as all the rich yuppies that live in my neighborhood. Seriously, if I see one more stay-at-home Trixie pushing her future alimony payment in an $800 stroller, there's going to be jail time involved. And don't get me started on the Range Rovers that are apparently a requirement to live here. . . .

Q: *Dude . . . the apartment?*
A: Sorry. The apartment is great. It's a two-bedroom in a three-flat that is joined with another three-flat. There are hardwood floors, a dishwasher, and two porches (one in back and one in front). Both will serve as excellent gathering spots. I live with an engaged couple—Dan and Anitra—who are both poke-your-eyes-out pretty. Our rent is $1,350, which, split three ways, isn't all that bad and is below the norm for a two-bedroom up here. We had a small dispute when I started displaying my gaudy collection of Elvis memorabilia, but that's about it. A bust of the King now sits on our mantel.

Q: *How close is it to Wrigley Field?*
A: It's less than a quarter mile northwest of the park. To get there just head up Clark Street and turn down Grace. Or head west on Waveland and north on Wayne. We live right behind a Dairy Queen. As if I didn't have enough problems maintaining a balanced diet.

Q: *How do you feel about the first month of the Cubs season?*
A: Well, after one month and twenty-four games, the Cubs have a middle-of-the-road 12–11 record. They've already suffered some injuries and have showed some of the mopey, uninspired play that ultimately doomed them in 2004. However, an entire season can't be judged on one month. Plus Derrek Lee has been unstoppable— he hit .419 for the month, including 7 home runs and 28 RBIs. Which has caused us all to say, Sammy who?

Chapter Five

A Brief Glimpse from Heaven...

May 6-8—vs. Philadelphia

Sue Ellen, the girl from the bar, comes through with her promise of rooftop tickets. That's just how it works with the Cubs sometimes. You run into somebody at a bar, they know a guy who knows a guy. Suddenly you're sitting six rows behind the visitors' dugout, courtesy of some rich jerk at some rich company. You find yourself sitting next to other rich jerks. But it's okay, you know, because you're at the Cubs game and it's probably free.

For the first (and hopefully last) time in my life, I find myself asking another man what I should wear to a baseball game. Yes, it's just a regular Friday at Wrigley, but it's also a corporate outing. Are we supposed to look like schmoozers? What's the best camouflage? A Nike golf shirt and khakis?

Brian says not to worry about it. A Cubs shirt and a pair of shorts should be fine. We're just going to a baseball game. Everything will work out. Wear whatever you want.

Brian, a college friend, is a drug rep for Pfizer and seemingly works less than I do. On the walk to Wrigley, he details the plan as issued by Sue Ellen. Technically, we're not supposed to be at this gathering, which is taking place at 3927 Sheffield. It's a client-only thing for her company, which is some sort of marketing firm. But our attendance should be no problem because Sue Ellen snuck us on the list. We'll be representing Wickes Furniture, a well-known company in Chicagoland. If anyone asks, we deal in dining sets and curio cabinets. (Admissions that will also make us seem extremely gay.)

A batch of conflicting feelings mixes through my churning mind. Lord knows how many times I've sat in the grandstand and wondered what it would be like to watch the game from the rooftops. In a few minutes, I'll find out. And since there will reportedly be unlimited food—beer, bratwurst, hamburgers and hot dogs—I intend to punish someone for making such a generous decision.

But there's also a nagging guilt, like I'm about to trade in my writing career for a three-piece suit and a corner office. Everyone knows these rooftops haven't been the same since the mid-'80s, when the profiteers first got the idea of charging people for access.

Climbing a rooftop and watching the Cubs used to be this great organic and spontaneous experience. Apartment dwellers on Sheffield and Waveland invited friends, then dragged rickety lawn chairs and cases of beer up the stairs. Once on the roof, residents listened and toasted their good fortune as Harry Caray called the action from the radio.

Innocently impromptu, you could call it.

That romantic notion has been tarnished by the pursuit of big bucks. The going rate is $150 (and sometimes more) per head to sit outside the field. Corporations with the ability to pay get most of the bookings. Building residents are allowed on the roof only one or two games per year, a small perk for renting. That doesn't matter much, though, because the number of tenants has decreased. Those third floors have been transformed from apartments into lounges and concession kitchens. The first floors and garden apartments are occupied, but I get the feeling that's only to preserve the buildings' residential zoning status.

The corporate junkets started in the mid-1980s when the building owners figured people would actually pay to watch from their property. Bleachers were erected and pregame menus were planned. When one of the landlords barred his tenants from the roof, the fans in the bleachers turned and chanted, "Landlord sucks! Landlord sucks!"

Now even the Cubs have their hand in the till. In 2002, the team put up dark-colored shades over the fences in left and right field, blocking most of the view for the enterprising rooftop owners. The shades only came down when an agreement was worked out—the Cubs receive 17 percent of the profits each season.

I'd bristle if ever labeled a purist. But in this case, guilty as charged. Something that was once wonderfully spontaneous has been ruined, at least partially. For the first time, I can sort of understand why those anti-everything hippies at UW threw bricks through the windows of the Gap on State Street.

Ten minutes later, I decide the rooftop money isn't all that bad. If the bucks weren't coming in, the rooftop owner would not be able to pay this beautiful, young, and nubile woman to check our names off a list.

Somewhere a salon is missing its shampoo girl.

The woman, who is sitting on the stoop with a clipboard, confirms that we are indeed on the list, then pulls out a digital camera.

"Get together, you two," she says. "We're taking a picture of everyone who comes into the party." (In twenty-four hours, someone at Sue Ellen's company will be checking the photo results and saying, "Hey, who are *these* guys?")

No matter. *Cheese!* The digital camera clicks.

We pass through the door and climb a giant wooden staircase, the type you might find in a faux-Irish bar, to the third floor. In the doorway, we make our first mistake, giving a slight pause that broadcasts a vibe of "Hey, we're not supposed to be here."

Our second mistake can be attributed to Brian: We are definitely underdressed.

Apparently my $25 cargo shorts from American Eagle, a Mark Prior number-22 jersey T-shirt, and four-year-old Birkenstocks are not appropriate for an event of this stature. Neither are Brian's flip-flops. The first lady I see is wearing a strand of pearls. Her husband is wearing a sport coat. I suppose, if you want to get into semantics, we are not actually at a baseball game. But, for the love of Sandberg, we're across the street from Wrigley Field! Surely that has to figure into any sartorial decisions.

Sue Ellen is handing out name tags near the back of the room. Safety. But before we can reach her, a man wearing a polo shirt with the company's name interrupts us. He is in his mid-forties. From the skeptical look on his face, it's apparent we look suspicious to him. To us, he looks like a major problem.

"Hey, guys," he says.

"Hey," we respond before realizing there is nothing else to add.

We awkwardly walk by the man and straight to Sue Ellen for our coveted name tags. Perhaps they will validate our presence and allow us to lie about working for a furniture company.

"Uh, guys, something came up," is the first thing Sue Ellen says. "The guys from Wickes showed up and we had to change the name of your company, so now you're working for Insignia."

"Okay," says Brian. "What does Insignia do?"

"Well, I'm not really sure," Sue Ellen says. "But just head upstairs to the roof. No one's going to bother you up there. . . ."

She motions to the lounge, where the suits are looking at some sort of—*what the hell?*—art show. It's doubtful they'll ascend to the roof anytime soon. "So just help yourselves to the food and the beer and I'll come up to see you guys later."

We are handed name tags and a lame party program that tells us about the company. Apparently, the top guy is known as the "Chief Imagination Officer." More like "Chief Dork."

After another flight of stairs, we find ourselves on the other side of the rainbow. We're looking back at Wrigley, which resembles a midsized canyon from our vantage point. The grandstand, especially the one that hugs Addison, looks a bit more dramatic up here. It is long and slowly filling. The field also looks more expansive. For the first time this season, the ivy on the walls is starting to resemble shag carpet.

This rooftop boasts one of the more intricate setups on Sheffield. The bleachers are double-tiered, and the wide metal beams are the highest on this side of the street. So this is what it's like to be Harry in heaven. You can't see the warning track in right field, but the entire scoreboard is visible. So are the bleachers; and at this moment two girls are leaning up against the chain-link fence.

In our rush to see Wrigley, we bypass the concession stand, which is just gearing up for the day. As promised: hamburgers, hot dogs, and brats. Brian and I decide to grab a beer. To toast our successful infiltration, of course.

But this is where my notes—and our rooftop blitzkrieg—end.

We turn, only to be greeted by the man with the company polo shirt. He followed us upstairs. It's just the three of us.

"Hey, guys, how you doing?" he says.

"Yeah, real good now," says Brian. For a moment, we turn back toward the railing and pretend to look at the field. An instant later, we wheel back and try to act professional, or at least like we belong there. John Goodman's voice from *Lebowski* rings in my head: *"DUDE! Are you fucking this up?"*

"Jeffrey, vice president of sales," says the man.

He extends his hand. I shake it and look him straight in the eye.

"Kevin Kaduk," comes out of my mouth.

"Brian," comes out of Brian's.

Maybe we can still rebound. To describe Jeffrey in one sentence: He shows an air of frustrated superiority that somehow suggests he hasn't been laid in the past fifteen years. Therefore he must be a real stickler for the rules, and probably derives pleasure from playing policeman at events like this one.

On the other hand, his apparent nerdiness could prove to be an asset. Maybe we can play buddies with him, make him overlook this invasion. Maybe he could use a few friends.

Or maybe not. Our presence is decimated with this simple exchange.

"So, who do you guys work for?"

"Insignia," Brian and I say, simultaneously.

"Oh yeah?" says Jeffrey. "Tell me, what does Insignia do?"

Uh, good question. I turn back toward the field so that Brian can handle this one on his own. A fit of laughter creeps up on me, but wait . . . yes, stifled just in time.

Brian, a loping six-feet-five redhead, quickly grows tomato-faced. He looks a bit like Conan O'Brien when the zookeeper brings his misbehaving animals on the set. Brian doesn't answer for five seconds. Then for ten. Then for fifteen. He sadly looks at me for help. But if there was ever a textbook case of throwing someone under the bus, this is it. I have no idea how to answer this question. Insignia? Never heard of it. You're on your own, Brian.

"Look," Brian finally says, "if you want us to leave, that's fine."

"That's what I thought," Jeffrey says. "Well, let me go check something and we'll see if this is a big deal or not."

No surprise. Jeffrey the Sniveler is going to hold us up as trophy bucks in front of his boss. It does not matter that his company is already dropping some nice coin on this whole shebang and probably paid a flat rate for the rooftop and won't be saving $300 even if we leave right now.

This whole situation is all about *Hey, look who I caught!* Instead of what it should be, namely, *Hey, guys, do you like the Cubs? Well, I like the Cubs. Let's be friends. You are certainly welcome to stay because we are a good company and I am not a stickler for the rules and everyone should enjoy the Cubs regardless if we have turned these rooftops into a breeding ground for corporate greed and customer bribery or not. Here, have a beer.*

Jeffrey heads downstairs as we await a near-certain fate.

"Maybe we should go try and drink as many beers as we can before he comes back," I suggest. "That'd show him."

Jeffrey is back within a minute.

"I'm going to have to ask you guys to leave," Jeffrey says. "This is a party for clients only. Our employees weren't supposed to invite their friends and—"

"Look, man," I say in a last-ditch effort to save our rooftop status, and maybe Sue Ellen's job. "I'm going to be honest with you. I'm writing a book and thought it would be cool if we were up here to experience such a unique part of Wrigleyville. We certainly appreciate your hospitality and we're not going to cause a—"

"I don't care."

His arrogance is startling. "Excuse me?"

"I don't care."

With that, we are gone, dumped down the back stairway that was erected just for the rooftops. Unfortunately our walk of shame doesn't wind past the art show and its pearl-wearing crowd. We could have made a scene. Instead the back staircase spits us out on ground level, in front of a group of twenty-somethings who seem surprised to see us leaving a game so early. The Cubs and Phillies are still twenty minutes away from the first pitch.

Maybe my expectations were different. In 1985, the author Bob Wood visited Wrigley on a cross-country ballpark tour for his book *Dodger Dogs to Fenway Franks*. On his second day in the neighborhood, he approached one of the Sheffield apartments and knocked on the door. "Can I watch from up on the roof?" he asked. "Go on up," said a building resident. Wood was, at first, ostracized by the regulars. Nontenants weren't normally allowed on the roof. But after sharing a gift of Old Style and imparting his knowledge of the Cubs, the fans quickly accepted him. Wood enjoyed the day, even having his author photo taken in a lawn chair with the exposed belly of Wrigley in the background.

Perhaps I thought Sue Ellen's company would act in a similar fashion: wary at first, then super-welcoming as the sunshine and beer seeped into the bloodstream. Except we were brushed aside in the rush to bolster business relationships that were probably already strong to begin with. The irony is that the only person wearing a Cubs shirt (me, as far as I could tell) was not welcome at the party.

We are too tired from laughing to deal with scalpers, so we head to the Full Shilling and order two pitchers of Miller Lite. (Later we'll scoreboard watch from the patio at Sports Corner.) The bar is empty, save for a Billy Bob Thornton type sitting on the next stool. It's Gar, who drives the equipment truck for Coldplay, who happen to be playing a sold-out show at the Metro later in the evening.

"Where did you guys come from?" he asks.

We were on a rooftop for ten minutes, we tell him.

Gar shakes his head.

"That's too bad," he says.

"It was a hell of a ten minutes though," Brian says.

May 9–11—vs. New York (NL)

Maese and Brewer are in Chicago for two games against the Mets. These guys are journalism heroes to sportswriters my age.

They're both in their mid-twenties and already hold columnist gigs at major newspapers (Brewer in Louisville; Maese is two months away from being hired in Baltimore). They did what I couldn't. Which is to say climb out of the journalism wading pool before a wave of high school ennui washed over their heads.

That they're both excellent writers, savvy networkers, and all-around good guys certainly helps. They have covered the 2004 Summer Olympics in Athens, the Super Bowl in Jacksonville, and about any other big event you can think of.

It's hard not to be envious of these guys, who I met through business but have come to consider friends.

Yet they, in turn, are jealous, at least a little bit, of my current lot in life. "Dude, you go to a Cubs game any day you want," says Maese, a Cubs fan who grew up in, of all places, Albuquerque. "Do you know how many people would kill to be in your spot? You're living the dream."

Appreciating the present has always been hard for me, a guy who immediately turns nostalgic for items once they enter my rearview mirror. That I'm attending Cubs games on a daily basis doesn't seem to run a continual register in the mind. It takes prompts—drinking heavily on a Monday night without regard for next-morning consequences, the hundreds of sweeties I see at Wrigley, getting booted off a rooftop—to trigger thankfulness. When I was staying with Jedd and Brian, they'd leave in the morning and head to their corporate jobs—and before they left, they instructed me to "have fun." How many people can say they're instructed to "have fun" at their jobs?

At the same time, after attending eleven of the Cubs' first twelve games, I can foresee a danger of it becoming routine. Going to Wrigley will be a onetime experience for a portion of the three million fans expected to pass through the turnstiles. They'll take pictures, buy T-shirts, spend more than they should on beer, and mingle around the neighborhood for hours after the game.

Now that I'm four blocks away, I can slip in five minutes before the national anthem and leave right after the final out. No pictures needed to prove I'm there, no cups of Bud to stretch the buzz to the hotel room.

So, the question becomes: Is a onetime experience more special than repeated visits to the same event? Perhaps it's a matter of perspective, but I'll side with going to as many games as possible.

Chad can't dig in his wallet fast enough. He pulls out five twenties without even looking at the two tickets I'm holding in my hand.

"Just fifty apiece? Really?" he asks. Trixie, who is wearing a black tank top and a white coffee filter of a skirt, hangs on to his arm. Going to a Cubs game is *sooo cool!* reads the look on her face. We are standing at the corner of Sheffield and Waveland, in front of Murphy's Bleachers, where there's always a nice flow on the secondary ticket market.

Normally I wouldn't think of selling extra tickets for over face value. But the circumstances somehow feel right. Maese was supposed to receive three tickets through a hookup. Only two were left. We have to find three together (only slightly less difficult than swimming across Lake Michigan), while selling the extra two at the same time. The two tickets have a face value of $27 apiece.

Not that I haven't mentioned it before, but here it is again: Like Opening Day Andy, I detest the put-together fratties and ready-for-a-Prada-runway bimbos who have seemingly gravitated toward Wrigley Field in the past few years. Damn right I'll sell these tickets to you for $23 over face, even though it's a buyer's market out here and you're too dim to figure it out. Listen, pal: Wrigley Field isn't a place to be seen, it's not a hard-to-get-into club, it isn't a place to talk on your cell phone. If you are not here to watch baseball, then I have no problem in taking your father's money. And with dopes like Chad around, it's no wonder that scalpers are making so much money.

With a hundred bucks in my pocket, we head south on Clark to a storefront scalper. Since he's the farthest away from the action, he's the first to drop prices. *Got three bleachers?*

"Yup, twenty bucks apiece," he says, discounting an immediate $10.

"The guy down there is selling them for seventeen," says Maese, his novice words infused with an admirable touch of deception.

"All right, fifteen dollars apiece," says the scalper, leaving us $55 extra for beer.

With the two out-of-towners in attendance on Tuesday, the Cubs win 7–0 for their second victory in three games. This is a welcome change. While the team was out of town, it dropped five straight games to Houston and Milwaukee. Then it came home and dropped two to Philadelphia before winning the series ender on Mother's Day. The streak is indeed troubling, and over beers at the Full Shilling we wonder what the season has in store for the Cubs, who are currently four games under .500. Maese says not to worry; it's still early.

Last January it seemed as if the arrival of baseball season would also bring a streak of great weather. Rainy and cold days would disappear with the first pitch of the season. Postcard blue skies would accompany the first seventh-inning stretch. As Chicagoans, we should have known better. With the exception of last night, there hasn't been an occasion to leave the long sleeves at home.

It is no different today, a Wednesday afternoon, for the series ender against the Mets. The wind is strong off Lake Michigan and the temperature evokes memories of mid-March. My game mate is Chris, a grade school friend and current Northwestern law student. I meet her near the park and we buy upper-deck box tickets for $10 (see a pattern here? An Alexander Hamilton can get you anywhere) and climb the ramps for the first time this season.

Unlike in most stadiums, the upper deck in Wrigley Field isn't a bad place to sit, so long as you avoid the poles in the 500 level. In many ways, the 400-level seats (the first ten rows of Wrigley's upper deck) are better than the 200-level terrace reserved seats. There's no grandstand to cut off the view, no poles to be stuck behind. Plus, it feels like you're on top of the action. Wrigley Field's upper deck ends where most parks' second tiers *begin*.

From our vantage point, everything is visible. We've got a good view down the first base line, plus we can see the bleachers, the scoreboard, and, best of all, the neighborhood beyond. It's like we're the king and queen of Wrigleyville.

Yet no amount of hot chocolate or 7-Eleven coffee can keep us warm. We rub our hands together. We stick them between our knees. The upper-deck wind stream is trying to put us down for the count. We last until the eighth inning and then retire to a television with pints of Bass in the warm confines of the Shilling. Chris and I watch as Derrek Lee hits a game-winning homer in the bottom of the tenth inning. Maese and Brewer appear a few minutes later, filled with emotion.

"You didn't stay?" Rick says.

"Too cold."

"But I'm from New Mexico and I made it through."

"Yeah, but we've got common sense."

The Cubs leave town for a five-game road trip with a record of 15–18, already six games behind St. Louis in the NL Central.

Chapter Six

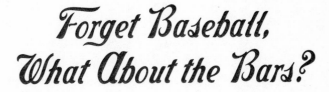

*Forget Baseball,
What About the Bars?*

Before each game, the perimeter of Wrigley Field becomes a mobile marketplace. Scraggly vendors roam the sidewalks, armed with knapsacks of merchandise and $75 licenses from the City of Chicago.

Peanuts? Three dollars for the small bag, four dollars for the big. Cheaper on the outside is one of sport's universal truths. Need Mardi Gras beads? A stuffed toy goat? A water-appliqué Cubs tattoo? Talk to Craig, a forty-something oddball who totes the junk around on weekends, trying to make a supplemental income with a laundry tub of memorabilia.

Everything is for sale. Cubs blankets, drawings of Wrigley Field and $8 pairs of sunglasses. The best sellers are the T-shirts, advertised three at a time by mounting mannequin torsos on long wooden poles. The slogans range from intra-city smack ("Sox Suck") to inter-city taunts ("St. Louis Sucks"), and from intoxicated boasts ("Drunk Chicks Dig Me") to Letterman-style lists ("Top 10 Lies Told at Wrigley"—"I'm not drunk"; "Parking's no problem"; "Our closer will stop them," etc.).

The funny part of it all is that you'll see a guy hawking a "Sox Suck" shirt one afternoon at Wrigley, and later you'll recognize him as he sells "Cubs Suck" shirts on the South Side. The lesson is not surprising. Capitalism trumps allegiance every time.

One of the most well-known shirts—"Shut Up and Drink Your Beer"—has always rubbed me the wrong way. The T-shirt's implication is, of course, that the action on the field is secondary to the drinking activity in the stands and bleachers. Go to enough games at Wrigley and you'll see this attitude displayed brazenly. Every so often a jackass will rise from his seat and announce to his section that he'll be watching the rest of the game from Murphy's or Sluggers or wherever, even if it's only the fifth or sixth inning. Each time, the jackass will flash a Cheshire smile and act like he's Joe Cool. Not even baseball can keep him from bellying up to the bar! It happens more than you think.

Don't get me wrong. Alcohol is absolutely a part of the Wrigley culture. Like dessert after a dinner date or wine during theater intermission, beer, for better or worse, is integral to the Wrigley experience.

Here's where I come down: Stay cool during the game, take back one or two Bud Lights, pay attention to the action and cheer. Afterward? Be my guest and go nuts. Run up an unsightly tab and worry about it when the Visa bill comes next month. Drink yourself into a coma, but try to avoid the dreaded "over-served" label. The bars in Wrigleyville are eagle-eyed for sloppy drunks.

After more than a month of making regular rounds around Wrigleyville (and also many other years of occasional visits), I feel qualified to weigh in on the topic of the neighborhood's refreshment depots.

It starts with the six "Disneyland" bars—Sluggers, Cubby Bear, Hi-Tops, Murphy's, Sports Corner, and Casey Moran's—thusly titled because they are crowded, overpriced, and, sooner or later, everyone ends up going there. You know, Wrigleyville obligation.

Apart from a brewery's worth of beer, it's unclear what these bars are selling each day. Are they pushing the image of the "neighborhood" bar where "regulars" come before Cubs games? Maybe.

But truth is that no one's a regular on game days. Everything at the Disneyland bars is designed so that the game-going cattle call can hand over its money as quickly as possible. *Step up to the bar. Two Miller Lites? Reach down. First motion. Crack (or Twist). Second motion. That'll be $9.50. Grab money. Third motion. Next person, please! Repeat until top of second inning. Take break. Resume pace after last note of seventh-inning stretch.*

You'd be sick if you knew how much the bars paid for the alcohol. It costs a bar in the area of seventeen cents for a twelve-ounce draft of beer. It's a little more for the can, but it's financially worth it. Bars can sell beers at a more rapid pace if they're cracking instead of pouring.

The bar does have expenses. Can you imagine the insurance policies these bars carry? Especially with some of their bathrooms inexplicably located down flights of stairs? Then there's the profit-sucking "friend of the bartender," who always stops by with a troupe of six or seven freeloaders. A few bars combat this by offering unadvertised $2 "friends of the bartender" specials. They're still making money.

But, for the most part, these bars are gold mines. And upon entering a packed bar after a win (or even a loss), I like to imagine that there's a small troll in the backroom, furiously turning the crank on a machine that prints nothing but hundred-dollar bills.

All the Disneyland bars have their special attractions:

• Casey Moran's was opened in 2004 by a group that owns five other North Side bars. Located due west of the park,

Moran's is the polished package, boasting twenty-five large plasma televisions and smooth wood furnishings. Moran's always seems to draw a crowd, and if you don't leave the game early, you're most likely standing in a line alongside Clark Street.

- Up the street, the Cubby Bear stands as the most recognizable of the Wrigleyville bars. It opened in 1953 and went through two different names—Cubs Pub and Cubs Grill—before the current moniker was chosen. Though a banner proclaims the Cubby Bear as America's "Great Neighborhood Bar," it's about the furthest thing from a tavern on the corner. The bar was remodeled in the off-season and now boasts over thirty thousand feet of drinking space and an accompanying restaurant named Vines. It's a decent place to watch live music, and off-their-prime bands (think Cracker or the Spin Doctors) play there all the time. Because of the music scene, the Cubby Bear is the most relevant Wrigley bar during the fall and winter.

- The Sports Corner, which hugs Sheffield and Addison, is run by George and Patty Loukas, who also own the Cubby Bear. Though the smallest of the Disneyland bars, Sports Corner boasts the best patio. Across from the bar rests the Harry Caray statue and right field gate. It's prime people-watching real estate, as the Addison El drops off just east of the bar.

- Home to the Opening Day Testicle Fiasco, Hi-Tops is probably the bawdiest bar in the district. Dark, low-lit, and not altogether pleasing to the eye, Hi-Tops is almost always the choice for the drunkest of the drunk, the crudest of the crude. It's true that the bar's waitresses are recognized as the best-looking in the neighborhood, but in that orange-skin, extra-skanky sort of way. Maybe it's just a coincidence, but Hi-Tops has been known as a favorite for visiting ballplayers and broadcasters. To this point, I've heard at least four over-the-line stories involving visits by players. Of course, like most bar behavior, the stories can't be confirmed.

• Though probably not the best of ideas, Sluggers combines two of the twenty-somethings' favorite activities: getting hammered and taking batting practice. There are several batting cages on the floor's second level, right next to a skee-ball setup and some random arcade games. In the next room, two guys play dueling pianos after every home game, which is perhaps the worst gimmick in Wrigleyville. You can only hear so many Journey impressions before throwing a pint glass at one of the offenders. Downstairs is a mess after every game, with wall-to-wall people in the sun-free area. It's not just a "Cubs" bar. Pick a night and there's a good chance that White Sox legend Minnie Minoso will be hanging by the bar. He lives nearby, just a few blocks from Wrigley, and is a regular.

Which brings us to Murphy's Bleachers, which ranks as the best Disneyland bar. It's not even close. When going out after the game, my jaunts always start at Murphy's. Located on Sheffield and Waveland and positioned like a tiny dog at the foot of the scoreboard, and the mouth of the bleacher entrance, Murphy's has been around in one form or another since the 1930s.

Ernie Pareti started the first business on the land, placing what he later said was a stolen hot dog cart on the corner. He served food from the cart and also beer by the pail, a beyond brilliant idea that has, for some reason, disappeared. Pareti named

the stand "Ernie's Bleachers." It remained there until the early
'40s, when Ernie built an actual tavern on the grounds. At the
end of World War II, Ernie sold the bar and it became "J.B.'s
Bleachers." A few years later, Ernie bought it back.

In 1965, Ray Meyer (not the DePaul basketball coach) bought
the bar and renamed it "Ray's Bleachers." This is when everything started to take off. In the late '60s, a group of bleacher regulars became renowned for their devotion and attendance to all
things Cub. The Bleacher Bums.

With the bar door exactly thirty-nine steps from the bleachers, Ray's became a natural postgame meeting spot for the Bums.
Some crew members worked there. Others just formed a three-
deep mob. Rumor has it that if you threw a shoe at a bartender, it
would be returned full of beer, along with a seventy-five-cent tab.

Over the years, Ray's became a special place, with its cramped
quarters serving as a meeting place for many. The backroom pool
table served as a game day condiment stand; ketchup, mustard,
and onions were spread on the table's green felt. Then the Cubs'
relative success in the '60s took a nosedive in the '70s and the
original Bums went their separate ways, blending back into the
mainstream of the regular world.

In 1980, Meyer finally gave into the persuasion of Jim Murphy, a former Chicago policeman who had been renovating apartments in the area and was looking for something bigger. At
thirty-one years of age, Jim Murphy bought the bar and "Ray's"
became "Murphy's."

Murphy immediately went to work implementing changes to
the decrepit and old Ray's. Murphy added a backroom, and the
east beer garden a year later. The famous sidewalk drinking area
was enclosed within a wooden fence, ensuring that no beer
drinkers wandered into the street.

The changes brought scorn from the old-timers who couldn't

accept change in their version of Wrigleyville. Jim Murphy was given the label of a bloodthirsty capitalist. In truth, Murphy and George Loukas were prescient, paving the way for Wrigleyville to become one of the top party spots in the nation. You can't help but look at the Cubs' $87 million payroll and think that both are at least a little responsible for the team's financial success.

Murphy kept making improvements over the years until early 2003, when he died from liver cancer at the age of fifty-four, just before the Cubs' ill-fated World Series run. His wife and sons now run the bar. On the corner light pole rests a brown sign that marks Sheffield as honorary "Jim Murphy Way."

Behind the Disneyland bars stands a crop of solid bench players, places to get away from the mobs and the noise if not necessarily the high prices. On the northern side of Clark, there's Bernie's Tap, the Full Shilling, Trace, and Raw. On the south end of the street, there's Ivy, Bar Louie, Goose Island, Irish Oak, and a few others. To escape the epicenter, one can always travel west to Southport, where a number of trendy bars have been erected in recent years—Messner's, Hye Bar, Neybour's, SoPo Grill, Mystic Celt, Cullen's, Justin's, Toons, the Schoolyard, Southport Lanes, and Blue Bayou.

It can be amazing to watch the postgame migration of the Wrigley crowd to the bars. This is because the crowds are never affected by a win or a loss. The Cubs could have just fallen 16–0 and Murphy's would still be packed. This fact would seem to contradict my claim that Cubs fans are invested in the outcome, but I see it differently. For many people, "going to a Cubs game" has come to mean a whole day's worth of events. And again, for many that list of events almost always ends with drinking seventeen beers before buying an $81 round of SoCo Limes for the eight Tennessee tourists you just met at Hi-Tops. Very rarely is a day at Wrigley followed by a fine dinner at Charlie Trotter's. If you only go to one or two Cubs games a year, it's possible you're going to drink more than a longshoreman.

"Give strong drink unto him that is ready to perish, and wine unto those that be of heavy hearts," reads the Book of Proverbs, chapter 31, verses 6 and 7. "Let him drink, and forget his poverty, and remember his misery no more."

This description certainly does not apply to the typical Wrigleyville drinker. Your typical imbibers here are in their twenties, upwardly mobile, relatively attractive, and overwhelmingly white. They hail from affluent suburbs like Grosse Pointe, Michigan, Barrington, Illinois, and Eden Prairie, Minnesota. Born on third base, there's little reason for the stupid amount of alcohol each privileged kid (including me) consumes over the course of the year.

Yet that's exactly what happens in Wrigleyville, which provides a college lifestyle for as long as anyone wants to live it. It can be boring and repetitive, but it is something to do. And who cares if you did the Wrigley drinking thing the week before? Lost in a cloud of booze, it can be hard to keep track.

Chapter Seven

Chicago's Uncivil War

May 20–22—vs. Chicago White Sox
May 23–25—vs. Houston Astros
May 26–29—vs. Colorado Rockies

One night, over a postgame drink at Murphy's, I find myself talking with a friend of a friend. Larry is in his mid-forties and by most accounts a general success in life. He has a high-paying job as a trader, good-looking children, and a second wife who might have been the inspiration for the term "MILF." He claims to be friends with Glenn Beckert, the second baseman from the '69 Cubs, and says that he once stared down Hall of Fame pitcher Bob Gibson (successfully) at a fantasy baseball camp.

As a kid, Larry used to head to Wrigley Field, where he was waved through the turnstiles a few innings into the game. When the day was over, he went through each aisle and flipped the seats to an upright position. The work earned him a free ticket to the next day's game.

Larry loves the Cubs. Goes to as many games as possible. He's devoted.

Yet despite that impressive résumé, one simple admission from Larry could earn him the distrust of fellow Chicagoans. Larry is also a White Sox fan.

To make such a confession in Chicago means becoming a city leper. It's probably better to declare loyalty to New York–style pizza or the Green Bay Packers. Liking the Cubs *and* the White Sox? *Nuh-uh*. Pick one.

For his part, Larry doesn't care about the looks he gets from friends, coworkers, and acquaintances. He can defend himself.

"I had an uncle who worked for WGN, and they broadcast both Cubs and White Sox games, so I saw a lot of games at each park," Larry says. "My dad owned a drugstore on the South Side, on Halsted, eight blocks from the White Sox and old Comiskey Park.

"Liking the White Sox and Cubs never used to be a problem in this town. They still play in separate leagues, but they never used to play each other. Since interleague play [in 1997], it's a lot different. Now it seems like you have to choose one."

So Larry, for the upcoming series, Cubs or Sox?

"I cheer for whoever's doing better, so I'll be rooting for the Sox. I know it sounds like I'm a fair-weather fan, but I grew up loving *Chicago*. I grew up loving *my teams*. Nobody is going to tell me I have to pick just one. I'm not afraid to say that I like the Cubs and the Sox."

There are Chicagoans who can sympathize with Larry. I am one of them. Maybe it's because we're already comfortably into this book, but I have no problem confessing this.

That's right: I also happen to like the White Sox as well as the Cubs. Watch them on television. Read the recaps in the papers. Turn the 'stiles at New Comiskey or "the Cell" (Chicagoans don't call it U.S. Cellular Field) more than a few times each season.

If you love baseball, what's the problem in liking both? The teams are in different leagues, play each other only six times a season (about 3 percent of the season), and hold their games at different times of the day. What other town can boast of following one team in the afternoon and then another at night? Two teams doubles the number of games one can watch to 324 per season. That might be a bit much, and as my roommate asked me when he got home from work the other night, "Is there going to be a time this summer when you're not watching baseball?" The answer was no.

As I lamented before, the city of Chicago has gone a combined *183* seasons without winning a World Series championship. The odds of this happening go beyond any sensible possibility. Why not double our chances, if not necessarily our pleasure or fun?

Let me put it another way. Say you own two three-legged horses and both are entered in the fifth the Kentucky Derby. Could you really cheer against one of them?

So how did this dual fanship happen?

Well, Mom and Dad grew up on the East Side of Chicago, a working-class neighborhood around the southern bend of Lake Michigan, near the steel mills and oil refineries that hug the Indiana state line. The neighborhood's residents were largely Eastern European. They got jobs, built churches, and bought affordable bungalows.

Neither of my grandfathers was a huge baseball fan. My paternal grandfather came to the United States from what is now Slovakia as a teenager, and was an Amoco employee for over forty years. Gymnastics was his interest. He was never a baseball expert, and when he began teaching me the game in his backyard, I was instructed to run left instead of right from home plate. Papa Charlie was confused, but when he watched the Sox one night, he realized his mistake and corrected my five-year-old self during the next day's lesson.*

---

*This, along with my inability to hit a curveball, general lack of athleticism, and dislike of chew, might explain why I am writing a book about baseball and not earning millions playing it.

My father became a Sox fan because that's where his father took the family to games. Hiking up to Comiskey was a long enough trip, so no way they'd truck all the way to Wrigley on the North Side. Somehow my uncle Chuck still became a Cubs fan, creating one of the brother versus brother rivalries you see all over this town.

When I came along, Dad packed me up in the big green Aspen station wagon and took me to old Comiskey Park at the corner of Thirty-fifth and Shields. Old Comiskey had worn and whitewashed walls, rickety green seats, and seemingly thousands of steel girders we could be stuck behind.

It also had a number of qualities a five-year-old might like: the scoreboard that exploded with fireworks every time a home run was hit, double-decked outfield roofs that provided Sox sluggers with inviting targets, and two big furry mascots—Ribbie and Roobarb—that rode into the stadium aboard a four-wheeler.

Ron Kittle, Carlton Fisk, and Harold Baines became instant heroes, taking their places alongside Big Bird and Mister Rogers. One of my earliest memories became playing catch with my father in the driveway while he explained that outfielder Rudy Law, with his seventy-seven stolen bases in 1983, was one of the fastest men in the major leagues.

At the time we lived in the small southern suburb of Hazel Crest, and, as such, we didn't make it to Wrigley Field much. While Dad is not anti-Cub ("I want to see them do well," he claims), he has never been a fan of Wrigley. Too cramped, and the lines for the bathroom are too long. Plus, where the hell do you park? New Comiskey, with its wide concourses and urinal trough–less bathrooms, is just fine, thank you. As a result, the number of times I've been to Wrigley with Dad can be counted on one hand.

He did take me to my first Cubs game, though. It was late in the summer of 1984 and the Cubs were charging to their first playoff experience since the 1945 World Series. The Cubs were a new thing to me. I discovered them in the way that many in my generation did. Each afternoon, I'd sit in front of the television and ready myself for an afternoon of cartoons on WGN. Every once in a while, at 1:00 p.m., a voice would come on and say something like, "We interrupt our regularly scheduled programming for this special presentation by WGN Sports."

Before I could consider my disappointment, a man came onto the screen. To a six-year-old, he was just another cartoon character. White hair. Thick, black glasses. Pleasant and old enough to be a third grandfather for every kid in the viewing audience.

"Hello again, everybody!" said the man, his shout barging its way into our family room and countless others across Chicagoland and the nation.

"And welcome to Wrigley Field on a beautiful day for baseball." This was much better than Heckle and Jeckle!

"Harry Caray here," said the man. "Along with Steve Stone."

For the next three hours, smack up to dinnertime, I was introduced to the Cubs by Harry Caray. In turn, I learned about a new cast of characters. Ryne Sandberg. Jody Davis. Gary "Sarge" Matthews. Ron "the Penguin" Cey. Bobby Dernier. Rick Sutcliffe. Dennis Eckersley.

And then there was the best supporting actor in the sports world—Wrigley Field, which then played all its games during the day and featured beautiful girls in the grandstands and tanned potbellied bums in the bleachers. Every so often—and these were my favorite days—Harry and Steve would call the game from center field. Harry would have his shirt off and would carry the same large fishing net he kept in the booth for errant baseballs.

Even then, you could tell there was something different about a broadcast from Wrigley. When a runner led off from first, the camera on the first base line clicked on, framing the theft-minded runner and the attentive first baseman against the backdrop of the left field ivy. When there was a bang-bang play at third base, the backdrop was the right field ivy and the Sheffield rooftops peeking over the stands. There was no advertising to ruin the scene, no artificial turf to suck the drama from a line drive that caught the home run basket in left.

Anyway, these images were with me when my father awoke me on a Saturday morning in July. We were headed to Wrigley with Dad's college buddy Tom and Tom's wife, Nancy. Perhaps planting a lifelong love of uncertain admission, we didn't have tickets to the game. No problem, said Dad.

When we got to the corner of Clark and Addison, Dad swept me up and placed me on his shoulders. He took his pointer and middle finger and showed me how to hold them toward the sky. The game was sold out and we'd need to look for tickets, he said.

"You should yell out, 'We need two!'" Dad instructed. "That'll help us get tickets."

And so I did. There are pictures in life that I'd like to have but don't—the exact moment I met a nice girlfriend, a big hit in Little League, playing baseball in the backyard with Papa Charlie, who passed away after the 1984 season. But, if I had a choice, I might pick a photograph from that scene outside Wrigley, my first *Field of Dreams* moment, a special time with Dad.

We found two pairs of tickets, one of which was in the not-fit-for-a-kid bleachers, so I spent the game in the grandstand with Nancy. She bought me peanuts and a hot dog. When I wanted to see catcher Jody Davis, the lady next to me let me look through her binoculars. During the seventh-inning stretch we looked toward the press box, where Harry Caray, the cartoon man, was leaning from the box and singing with us.

I don't remember the team that the Cubs played (my best guess is Atlanta) or even if they won. But from that day on, I was hooked on the Cubs. Twenty-one years and much heartache later, the benefits of this addiction remain debatable.

*   *   *

On Friday morning, I head to Wrigley Field for the first of six meetings between the Cubs and Sox. The two teams are in decidedly different places. The Sox are 29–12, tops in the major leagues, thanks to firebrand manager Ozzie Guillen and the team's new focus on pitching and fundamentals.

The Cubs, meanwhile, are 18–20 and coming off a 3–2 road trip to Washington and Pittsburgh. The situation has lessened the importance of the crosstown series, and the scalpers say they are feeling it in their pocketbooks. "Worst situation for the Chicago series ever," says one of the brokers with an Addison storefront.

But you've got to give credit to both teams, they know how to play this series up. The teams don't do much clichéd ass-kissing through the media. For example, Guillen has constantly complained about playing at Wrigley this week. He says he doesn't like the cramped clubhouses or the dugouts or the showers. He related a story about getting lost on his way to Wrigley one day.

Most of all, as he's said this week, he doesn't like the parking situation. Last season he was directed to park at the McDonald's on Clark. Guillen isn't letting anyone forget about it.

"[Wrigley] is a beautiful thing to have in Chicago," Guillen told the press one day. "If you come to Chicago and don't come to Wrigley, it means you didn't come to Chicago. It's like going to New York and not seeing the Statue of Liberty.

"[But] if you come to work here, it's uncomfortable."

I walk north down Clark Street. One of the restaurant marquees displays a message that cannot be disputed. GOD BLESS THE SUNDRESS reads the board, and the steadily improving weather seems to agree.

At the corner of Clark and Waveland sits a vendor selling white T-shirts. They read CHILL, with a vertical City of Chicago flag taking the place of the "I." As streams of Cubs and Sox fans walk by, it's a message that should be heeded.

A good rivalry is never a bad thing, but the relationship between Cubs and Sox fans has taken a nasty turn over the years. Like the partisanship that bitterly divides the country, a baseball rivalry has threatened, to a much lesser degree, civic unity in Chicago.

Good-natured ribbing is gone, replaced by crude slurs that categorize, demean, and dismiss people.

To some Cubs fans, Sox supporters are nothing but "criminal white trash" who live in trailer parks, wear mullets, and run onto the field to attack umpires and first base coaches.* How do they know? Because the South Side is decidedly more working-class than the North.

And because the attendance at Sox Park comes nowhere close to Wrigley's total of three million, it stands to reason that Sox fans are not as loyal as the Cubs faithful. Also, the Sox play in a dangerous neighborhood (Bridgeport), and to see a game on the South Side is to risk your life, even if the streets around the stadium are lined with police officers and the high-rise projects have been knocked down.

On the flip side, Sox fans consider their North Side brethren to be drunken trust funders with no interest in the game that is being played before them. The Cubs are only popular because of the bars around Wrigley, which actually isn't the name of the stadium at all. Sox fans refer to Wrigley as "the Urinal" on most message boards, and God forbid if they step foot in it when the Sox aren't playing the Cubs. To be a Sox fan means making peace

---

*A September 2002 incident in which a drug-addled father and his teenage son rushed the field and attacked then–Kansas City coach Tom Gamboa gave rise to this stereotype. Yet Cubs fans fail to bring up similar incidents at Wrigley, such as the time in 1995 when a fan ran onto the field to confront reliever Randy Myers.

with the venomous and overly defensive core of Pale Hose fans who can't stand the recent wave of popularity the Cubs are enjoying. To these fans, the *Tribune* is the "Cubune," the *Sun-Times* is the "Cub-Times," and everyone is out to get the poor, poor White Sox.

There is some truth in all the above statements, but for the most part, they remain stereotypes. Ask a Sox fan, the business owner who has a massive spread in Orland Park, if he's white trash or a criminal. Ask a Cubs fan, the Ravenswood machinist who's only at Wrigley with his kids because someone gave him free 500-level tickets, if he's living high on the hog these days.

Up until recently, the city's dominant team has been a rotating title. Before the '90s, when everyone decided that Wrigley was a national treasure, the team with the better record usually decided attendance superiority. The White Sox owned the town in the '50s and '60s when they battled (usually unsuccessfully) the Yankees for the American League pennant. The Cubs regained the crown in 1969 and held it until the South Side Hit Men came along in 1977.

Now the city is definitely a Cubs town, with the 2003 season, Harry Caray, Sammy Sosa, and national exposure on WGN all playing equal roles. And because Guillen's quote about no visit to Chicago being complete without a trip to Wrigley is true, it seems the Cubs' stranglehold on the town's loyalty seems indestructible.

Still, I like both teams. Homesickness and affection for Chicago drew me back from Kansas City, and what good would hating even one aspect of the city do? The yin and yang of North and South Siders makes up an important part of the city's fabric. And because I don't have reason to hate either side, all the vitriol seems excessive. Call me a two-timer or call me indecisive. Just don't call me a man who doesn't love his city.

* * *

It's official. Dan is now my sugar daddy. We've got terrace box seats, just to the left of home plate and close enough to toss a ball to the home plate umpire.

There's a good mix of Sox and Cubs fans, but the North Siders still dominate. Last night, a man from a ticket agency was on television bemoaning the fact that the series wasn't selling well. He seemed sad. This is the easiest ticket in the eight-year history of the interleague series, he claims.

The interest would undoubtedly be higher if the Cubs were off to a better start. There's a certain caution in Wrigleyville right now. Everyone wants a reason for hope, maybe a seven-game winning streak to zero sum the losing streak that ushered in the month of May.

The Cubs side is quiet, but that changes in the first when Greg Maddux hits Sox rookie Tadahito Iguchi with an errant pitch. There's a slight buzz in the stands, and when Sox pitcher Freddy Garcia responds in the bottom of the inning by brushing back leadoff hitter Jerry Hairston, it grows a bit more. Two batters later, Garcia tattoos Derrek Lee's ribs with a fastball. Chicago's uncivil war begins.

And yet no one tells the Cubs. The Sox score one in the third and three in the fifth, and Jermaine Dye homers in the eighth to cement a 5–1 win in the opener. Garcia goes seven innings, allowing the Cubs only one run on five hits.

Afterward, I meet up with my brother Dave and his boss, Mike. We sit at a back table in Messner's, eating mini-corndogs and drinking Newcastles. Mike is a Sox fan and swears he never comes to Wrigley unless the Sox are playing. Even then, he doesn't like it. Dave, who tilts toward the Cubs, tones down his act when Mike is around. Later in the season, Dave will wear a Sox hat when Mike takes us to Sox Park for a company outing.

*　*　*

Chicagoans are a funny bunch. I'm not sure you'd find a bigger city that's more provincial. People grow up here and never leave. When we do, all we talk about is home. We carry a swagger and bravado that's one step below a New Jersey guido and one above a proud Bostonian. Outsiders suggest we use these boasts to mask our insecurities about New York, but when they say that, we just scoff. Chicago is a clean New York, we respond. And while we know that New York *might* be a little better than here, we're not going to admit it.

"Show me a kid from Chicago who says it *isn't* modern-day Rome and I'll show you a liar," I was once told by an acquaintance. There's a lot of truth in that statement. One of us leaves the city and we talk ad nauseam about the beautiful lakefront and the great museums and Wrigley Field and our Super Bowl champion Chicago Bears (no matter they won twenty years ago). In Kansas City, I preached so continuously that I was asked more than once if I "was ever going to shut the fuck up about Chicago?"

Whatever. I liked talking up my city.

See, Chicagoans are proud of our city and our sports teams, no matter how much they let us down. We're particularly proud of what's been done to our city in the '90s, the way the lakefront has come together with the opening of Navy Pier and the real estate growth on the North Side. We get things done, and when an out-of-towner says, "Oh, I *love* visiting Chicago," it doesn't come as a surprise. We're a bunch of people in the middle of America who have overcome the Great Fire, Prohibition gangsters, and Dennis Rodman to blossom into a world-class city. Can you blame us for bragging?

Despite our overwhelming provincialism, we are definitely a fractious family. There's a certain pecking order when it comes to the citizens of Chicago. On Saturday morning, I find myself in the Full Shilling, talking about this order with Jeff and Bill, two guys originally from Naperville who went to the University of Indiana and now live down the street from me. I had never met them before today, but twenty minutes after introductions we're talking like old friends.

Together, we decide the Chicago citizen hierarchy looks like this:

PEOPLE WHO ARE ACTUALLY "FROM THE CITY"

It may come as a surprise to some of the relocated college grads, but some people actually grew up in Chicago and came of age while riding the El and eating at Demon Dogs, a now-defunct hot dog stand underneath the tracks at Fullerton. These guys (who include my friend Haydn) know the city down to the sewers. They know which aldermen wield the real power, the best hole-in-the-wall Mexican joints, and the Sheridan Road bus schedule. The guys on the South Side know the best place to stop for early-morning coffee, which bars belong to the firemen and which belong to the cops, and the best places to get free parking around Sox Park. These guys went to private schools like Gordon Tech and De La Salle and probably would never think of setting up shop in my yuppie neighborhood.

THE SUBURBAN REFUGEES

Here's where Jeff, Bill and I fit in. When we're in another city and someone asks where we grew up, all three of us agree the answer is always "Chicago." When a more exact location is requested, we say "West Suburbs," to which the questioner will almost always reply, "Then you're not from Chicago!" Okay, you got us. Should we have said Chicagoland? Maybe we're not Chicagoans in the truest sense of the word, but most of us certainly feel it. We've had parents grow up in the city, and when they got a little cash, they headed to the burbs, which is what you did when you got a little cash in the 1970s. To the suburbanites, there really is no difference between the suburbs and the city. We just call the city part "downtown." The born-and-bred city dwellers will disagree, but I always felt like a Chicagoan. Lord knows I spent enough time at Wrigley and Comiskey and with my grandparents on the East Side to qualify. Though I will defer to the true city folk, out of respect. "We're definitely Chicagoans now," Jeff points out.

THE PERMANENT TRANSPLANTS

These are the people in the early or late thirties who moved to Chicago after graduation and haven't moved. Maybe they made a little money in the buildings downtown or maybe they've become a part of the artistic or writing community. Either way, they're not budging. They like everything about the city, contribute to the scene in positive ways, and don't make a spectacle of themselves. They blend in, act like Chicagoans, and are accepted. That's one of the best things I like about this town—once you're in, you're in.

THE CHADS AND TRIXIES

Maybe you think I'm overdoing this "Chad and Trixie" thing, but trust me, no one likes this section of Chicago. They're temporary citizens, only here for a few years to act like Carrie Bradshaw before heading back to Des Moines or the suburbs so they can play house with the prerequisite two SUVs in the garage or whatever. The infusion of their disposable income can probably be directly traced to the price hike in apartments, drinks at bars, and, worst of all, Cubs tickets. If it wasn't for their materialism, we would not be able to buy $72 vintage tees from the "boutique" down the street from my house. I know what you're thinking: *If they're going to move away in a few years, what's the big deal?* Well, it's like having a roach problem; there's too many sororities preaching groupthink and sending waves to Chi each spring. Sometimes it makes me want to eat my shoes.

* * *

Carlos Zambrano starts the second game against the White Sox, in front of 39,461 fans. Despite Mark Prior's promise and Kerry Wood's occasional scrapes with greatness, Zambrano has been the most consistent of the Cubs starters. He has a fiery temper that sometimes gets the best of him, but at least it is a visible passion, which is more than you can say for most of the current group of automatons in the Cubs dugout.

Zambrano owns the White Sox like Freddy Garcia did the Cubs in game one. The Sox go scoreless for the first seven innings and manage only three hits, while the Cubs take a 1–0 lead. Everyone knows that Zambrano can go the distance, but if the game gets turned over to the bullpen, it's going to be dicey. And so it happens. Zambrano gets pulled in the bottom of the seventh for a pinch hitter, and the Sox fans in attendance, about 30 percent of the crowd, suddenly stir optimistic. Cubs fans, meanwhile, wait for disaster.

I'm rooting for the Cubs, for reasons opposite of why Larry, mentioned at the beginning of this chapter, roots for the Sox. The Cubs need a win. The Sox could be swept and they'd still be atop the AL Central. If the tables were turned, I might root for the Sox, because there's no place like Chicago when both teams are in the hunt. In 2003, both teams were in contention until the Sox folded late against the Twins. The dual chases were so newsworthy that the Bears' training camp barely registered as a blip on the sports media scene.

Reliever Michael Wuertz enters the game in the top of the eighth and the crowd gets set for the outcome. On my right, I've got two Sox fans, a retired professor and his wife. On my left is a family of Cubs fans from a town near Terre Haute, Indiana. There are thousands of similar situations around this park. Wuertz gets the first out, but then Sox speedster Scott Podsednik legs out an infield single. He steals second before the next batter, Willie Harris, grounds to short for out number two.

The crowd is standing as Aaron Rowand comes to the plate. The center fielder gives more hope to Sox fans, hitting a grounder to deep short for the inning's second infield single. Runners on first and third, two outs.

Wuertz faces Paul Konerko, and everyone in Wrigley knows that this is the game, right here. Everyone's shouting at full volume and, for a moment, the game seems like the most important thing in the world.

The Sox fans kick in—*Pauw-lee! Pauw-lee! Pauw-lee!*

The batter and pitcher face off to a full count, and on the decisive pitch Konerko lifts a pop fly to short center field. Here's Corey Patterson, charging from the deep recesses of the park to make a play. A collective city breath is held. Patterson is motoring over as the ball makes its descent.

At this moment, with my heart pushing up against my Adam's apple, giving up my job in Kansas City and moving back turn completely worth it.

The crowd looks at the ball in the sky. Then at Patterson.

Back to the ball in the sky. And then back to Patterson again.

Patterson dives because it's necessary, not because he's trying to make ESPN's Web Gems, like Jim Edmonds does sometimes. With an outstretched glove, Patterson makes a forward flop and gets his glove on the ball.

From the Cubs fans, a Howard Dean scream: *Yeeeeaaaaaaaaaa-ahhhh!!!!*

The Sox fans wilt and stop cheering, but only for an instant, because it looks like Patterson closed his glove too early. The ball—along with the Cubs' lead—bounces away into the green carpet around the center fielder. Podsednik crosses home plate, and Rowand comes barreling around third for a 2–1 White Sox lead.

Now the Sox fans are screaming *Yeeeeaaaaaaaaaaahhhh!!!!* while the Cubs fans place theirs cupped hands over to their noses and mouths. The Sox score twice more in the inning (and once in the ninth), providing enough insurance for the two runs the Cubs will score in the bottom of the eighth.

White Sox 5, Cubs 3.

As I walk west on Grace Street, I recognize two people standing on the corner of Lakewood. The Cubs jersey–wearing pair had been jawing at Wrigley with a group of Sox fans. At one point, the guy wearing an Aramis Ramirez jersey charged down the steps and challenged a guy wearing a Konerko jersey to a fight. These guys were clearly from the city; they were wearing gold chains, and I suppose it's possible that everyone involved was a gang member. But Wrigley Field security, to their credit, recognized the problem and broke it up before any punches were thrown. The two groups screamed at each other for the rest of the game, with the surrounding sections watching with a certain sense of dread and fascination.

Drawing closer, I recognize the guy wearing the Ramirez jersey. Blood is dripping down his face and he's got the look of a bull that's just been stuck in the side. I think about asking him what happened, but decide against it. A GMC Jimmy pulls up and the pair jump in. The truck peels south down Lakewood, presumably to resume the fight that began in the stands. Who said it was just a game?

For Sunday's series finale, I discover the formula for a Cubs victory over the Sox—not showing up. I try to find a ticket, but I'm scalping with Art and Angie, and finding three seats together always presents a certain challenge. So after striking out, we sit on the curb outside the left field fence on Waveland Avenue and follow the game from the scoreboard on the façade. Prior salvages the series with a complete-game 4–3 victory over the Sox. Rookie

Jason Dubois hits a three-run homer to right, and the sanity of Cubs fans is somewhat restored.

In the future, my not showing up seems to work for the Cubs. When the team travels south to the Cell in June, I attend the first game, a 12–2 loss. Graduation parties prevent me from attending the last two, and the Cubs win both, forcing a series split in the Crosstown Classic. Of course, the presence or absence of one fan doesn't determine the fate of a team. But with the Cubs holding a 19–22 record, it's hard to believe I haven't started a jinx somewhere along the way.

Frequently Asked Questions

June

Q: *Have you interviewed any Cubs players yet?*
A: Nope. When I was a newspaper reporter, I talked with several Cubs and some opposing players about Wrigley Field. No one really had anything interesting to say past the usual lines, "Wrigley is beautiful" and "Cubs fans are great." You can't blame them though. With the exceptions of Kerry Wood and Corey Patterson, no current players were on the Cubs' roster in 2000. There's a lot of turnover, and players are usually going to say some nice things about their current team. That's not to say major leaguers don't love Wrigley; Chicago is usually ranked as the top place to play whenever they do those player surveys. But like I said before, this book is about being a Cubs fan. Rosters change. Hometown allegiances don't.

Q: *Are you going to enter any games with a press pass?*
A: Are you kidding? The Cubs don't even know I'm writing this book, which is how it should be. Knowing the Tribune Company, they'd want 17 percent of all my profits. The team has always been a master of spin (dating back to P. K. Wrigley's insistence on calling it "*beautiful* Wrigley Field"), and it's better to stay away from the doctors. Best to keep a clear mind and not even sample red-and-blue Kool-Aid.

Q: *So you're not going to enter the Cubs' locker room? That's too bad!*

A: The truth comes out. You want to hear about the locker room in Wrigley Field. Imagine a very long, fluorescent-lit hallway. Install thick lockers on both sides and place long folding tables in the middle. Then add a couple dozen players, coaches, and support staff. A few hours before the game, the media enters and it's even more cramped. The media has nothing to do but stand around and wait until whoever blew the game the previous night decides to come out of the training room. The logistics create a tense situation, and while I'm not condoning his whining, you can sort of see why Dusty Baker is always complaining about the Chicago media.

Q: *What has been the best part of the season so far?*
A: Unquestionably, it has to be the trade the Cubs pulled on May 28 when reliever LaTroy Hawkins was sent to San Francisco. *Arrivederci*, LaTroy! While Hawkins was a superb setup man for the Twins in 2003, he never adapted to the closer's role in Wrigley Field. He blew several saves down the stretch in 2004 and then a few in 2005. His attitude has never been a favorite of the fans or the media. As such, an air of bitterness existed for Hawkins every time he took the field. And while it's a strange feeling, I can't help but feel that we were subliminally rooting *against* Hawkins in his relief opportunities. Now that he's gone, we can turn our full attention to the players we *do* like. Strange.

Q: *What's been the worst?*
A: Another easy one. Thursday, May 27, 2:21 p.m. Rockies in town. In the top of the fourth inning, Brad Hawpe

drills a line drive off Mark Prior's elbow. Prior falls to the right of the mound while clutching his pitching arm. I'm sitting about thirty rows behind home plate, and while Aramis Ramirez picks up the deflected ball and makes a great play to throw Hawpe out at first, no one is cheering. Prior comes off the field, and all anyone can think is that we won't see him again this season. He was hurt coming into the last two seasons, and while a subsequent MRI was encouraging, we still won't be seeing him for a while.

Q: *So does the Prior injury and that Sox series spell premature doom?*

A: One of the things Prior did before his injury was to infuse a bit of much-needed enthusiasm in the Cubs. After finishing the Sox series with that Sunday win, the Cubs ended the month by taking five of seven from the Astros and Rockies and then sweeping the Dodgers on the road. The team started June by winning three of four in San Diego. Derrek Lee is having the best season of anyone in the majors, and the Cubs are returning for a nine-game home stand with a 30–25 record. The absence of Wood and Prior is a bit unsettling, but if we didn't have anything to worry about, would it really be baseball season?

Chapter Eight

*Summer Begins
and a Nation Invades
from the East...*

June 6–8—vs. Toronto

Finally, summer. I've got to be honest. Wearing sweatshirts to games in late May was starting to bother me. When you're sitting in the stands in the cold and the Cubs are playing below expectations, you start to wonder why you quit your job to sit here day after day. Cold is cold. Bad baseball is bad baseball. Even if you're sitting in Wrigley Field.

But walking up Addison Street on a warm Tuesday night, there's a feeling of rebirth. A black limousine, one of those gaudy jobs that's supposed to look like an H2 or a Lincoln Navigator, passes by. Four guys in their thirties are popping out of the sunroof, and while they look silly, it's hard to be cynical about them. Each one has a beer in his hand, and as the limo nears Clark and Addison they're singing along with the stereo at the top of their lungs. *"Hey Chicago, whaddya say? The Cubs are going to win today!"*

It's impossible not to feel upbeat when hearing this song. And considering the Cubs' dismal history, having an eternally optimistic ditty on hand seems a convenient way to snap out of a losing-induced funk. The song was written by Chicago's own

Steve Goodman, an over-the-top Cubs fan and songwriter who died of leukemia just weeks before the playoffs in 1984. More than twenty years later, "Go Cubs Go" plays countless times on any given day in Wrigleyville. Like most sports-related songs, it gets better with every beer.

There's a crowd around Wrigley's front entrance, but I don't have to bother with that tonight. Nor with the scalpers. Adam, one of my friends from college, has come through with tickets to another Sheffield rooftop.

Again, technically, I'm not invited to the party. But my name is on the list and Adam guarantees I'll be fine. He works in the advertising world, and tonight's party is being thrown by *Car and Driver*. Adam's company is one of their clients. When we get to the front stoop (and another amazingly attractive woman), Adam sees the chief party thrower and introduces me. Welcome, he says, and we head upstairs. God bless corporate outings.

This is the aforementioned *"Eamus Catuli"* (Let's go, Cubs) rooftop, just two buildings down from the scene of last month's ejection. The *Eamus Catuli* sign also reads "AC 026097." The message is cryptic but easily explainable. "AC" stands for *"Anno Catuli,"* translated from Latin as Year of the Cub. The following six digits are then broken up into two-digit increments:

- 02 years since the Cubs' last division title (2003)
- 60 since the last National League pennant (1945)
- 97 since the last World Series title (1908).

When the Cubs finally break through to win the World Series, the sign will presumably read "AC 000000," though winning through a wild-card berth would keep the first set of numbers the same. I think we'd still take it.

We reach the top of the stairs, turn left, and are greeted by a bar.

"I'll have an Amstel . . . ," I say before stopping to smile at one of the women behind the bar.

It's Cheyenne.

A month ago, I met Cheyenne through a mutual friend. We were at a birthday party at a swank restaurant in the Bucktown neighborhood, and both of us were stuck at the same end of the table. This led to some small chitchat, a few laughs, and a feeling at the end of the night that I had generally done a good job of (maybe) impressing her.

Let's get a confession out of the way. I am terrible at picking up women. I'm always apt to say something dumb or make a misstep or ask for her phone number too soon or too late. Think of a dating transgression and I've committed it. I'm the Jeff George of daters. No matter how many times I fail, there's always another chance to show my ineptitude.

Upon meeting Cheyenne for the first time, my initial urge was to ask if her last name was Wyoming. Miracle of miracles, I kept my trap shut and dutifully listened as she went on to detail her career.

While there is no postcollegiate question more loathsome than "So what do you do?," Cheyenne actually had a compelling answer. She is an actress based in Chicago. Her biggest break to date has been an Empire Carpet commercial,* and since she's of South American descent, she also starred in the Hispanic version of the commercial, doubling her bucks. Cheyenne currently has a walk-on role in a play, and when she's not doing that, she's tending bar on this rooftop.

"It's an easy job plus it's pretty fun," says Cheyenne, boiling her job down to the following responsibilities: opening beers, pouring wine, and smiling at shit-faced businessmen.

---

*Empire Carpet commercials are so prevalent in Chicago that many children—including myself—learn the company's number (Five-eight-eight, two-three hundred . . . Empp-iiire!) before their own.

For the job, Cheyenne is wearing her jet-black hair pulled back in a ponytail, dark sunglasses, and a green shirt that's tucked into khaki shorts. For a more accurate picture, think of the beer cart girl at an upscale golf course.

So, how do I play this? I ask myself. She's serving me beer and there are two coworkers on either side, so asking for her phone number seems out of the question. And what's the tipping situation? My first instinct is to give her twenty dollars *just because*. But everyone always says I'm too nice . . . maybe I should just leave her a note and nothing else? *Hey, sweetie, here's your tip— avoid touchy-feely agents. Smell you later. Love, K-Rock.*

And so goes my analysis. Adam and I head back downstairs to order food, a rather dry Italian beef and a so-so hot dog, from the kitchen. Issues of *Car and Driver* are spread across the tabletops. Several female ad reps arrive, all dressed like the woman on the cover of *The Devil Wears Prada*. Wouldn't want to be caught dead in Wrigleyville without your Louis Vuitton bag, right?

Adam's postcollege story is similar to mine. After graduating from Wisconsin, Adam headed to Detroit for a job with an advertising company. He wanted to advance his career and was determined to make it happen no matter where he had to go. A year into the job, Adam was diagnosed with testicular cancer. He went through chemotherapy and made all of us proud by whipping its ass. After recuperating, Adam refocused on his work. Except he didn't like living in Detroit, away from the action and the scores of young people he was used to. His job wasn't worth hanging out and growing old in places like Farmington Hills. So Adam took a lesser job in Chicago and doesn't see himself leaving.

"I'm obviously not from Chicago, but I've only been here a year and already I'm proud to say that I live here," says Adam. "I see this city as a place where you can make anything happen . . . do whatever you want to do."

Everyone around us—mostly young and well-dressed professionals—probably feels the same way. There is a certain swagger to the yuppies down here. It is a capable bunch—smart and privileged and seemingly invincible. You want disposable income? We'll give you disposable income. Ever wonder why the prices at Wrigley are so high? Take a look around you. *We have purchasing power and we're not afraid to show it. Nine bucks for a Stoli and soda? Here, take this ten spot. I am tired of carrying it around.*

The Cubs and Blue Jays begin play, and immediately there's a sense of detachment. We're at the game, but *not* at the game. It's actually more like a party with a really great view. We try to sit in a few of the blue bleachers up top, but all the seats are filled. Instead we stand on a stairway and watch the game on television. There's a few-second delay, so when there's a bang-bang play, we hear the roar before we see the action on television.

Being on a rooftop is okay, but you wouldn't want to watch an important game from this vantage point. The unlimited beer and food are a definite plus, especially when advertising money is picking up the tab. But given the choice, I'd rather be inside the walls of Wrigley.

If we were inside, we wouldn't be missing the headline from tonight's game. In the middle of the sixth inning, a black cat leaps from the stands, runs up the third base line, and leaps over the brick wall near the Cubs' dugout. The Cubs go on to lose 6–4, their second defeat in a row, and the cat's appearance makes everyone painfully recall 1969, when a black cat dashed its way past Ron Santo in the Shea Stadium on-deck circle. The Cubs went on to blow a five-game September lead, finishing eight behind the Mets in the standings.

Back on the rooftop, I've got to decide what to do with Cheyenne. We've conversed a few times when I've gone to the bar for a round of beers, but none of the coworkers have left her side. So instead of getting some courage, I rationalize that a third "random" meeting will be the best time to ask for her number. There's a good chance I will see her again.

I say my good-byes, drop a ten in her tip bucket and head home.

Two months later, I will talk to Cheyenne's friend and ask about her. There never was a third random meeting.

"Cheyenne? Oh, she got a new boyfriend. I think they're getting pretty serious." Timeliness has never been my strong suit.

It's visiting season. Since Monday, I've had two twenty-one-year-olds sleeping in my living room. They are friends of my roommate Dan's brother and they needed a place to crash. They say—*say*—they're leaving on Thursday. We'll see if that actually happens.

If you live in Chicago and it's summer, weekend visits are a constant. Everyone wants to be here for the summer so visits are announced, Cubs tickets are requested, and the alcohol tab grows larger and larger as the weeks go by.

Matt and Cole are from Omaha. They are driving around the Midwest, "seeing the sights." So far, this goal has only been achieved by sitting on our screened-in porch and smoking a supply of pot that would cripple an NBA team. They're like Penn and Teller. Every so often, the guy who talks (Matt) will emerge from the porch and ask questions, like "This Mayor Daley you have . . . is that the same guy from the sixties?" and "How do you get to Milwaukee?" Then he returns and relates the news to the guy who doesn't talk (Cole, who resembles a young John Turturro). Then they pack another bowl, smoke and sit in silence. From the other room, I have a flashback: It's junior year and I'm sitting in a Columbus, Ohio, hotel room with the photography editor from the *Badger Herald*. He is stuffing a towel under the door while insisting that he sees Thomas Jefferson outside our window. Meanwhile I'm trying to figure out how to charge pornography to our expense account.

But I digress. On Wednesday, I finally flush the Stoner Twins from our apartment.

"You guys want to go to the Cubs game?" I ask. "They're playing Toronto and it's a one twenty start."

"Depends. Can we smoke up first?"

"I guess so."

An hour later, I enter the bleachers with two stoners. They head to the concession stand while I claim the usual seats in the third row. Is drug use common at Wrigley Field? I can't say, though a few years back I sat behind a thirty-two-year-old man who was tripping on ecstasy. He left in the third inning and looked near death.

Behind us is a group of four guys. Each has painted a C, U, B, or S on his bare chest. They're from Omaha, too, and are in town for this weekend's much-anticipated interleague series against the Red Sox.

"We don't have tickets yet," says one. "We're hoping to get lucky. Something will work out."

Closer to center field sits another group of guys. Each has a D, L, E, or E on his chest, in honor of first baseman Derrek Lee, who is currently in Triple Crown contention with a .378 average, 17 homers and 52 RBIs. Midway through the first, the "D" gets a tap on his shoulder from Wrigley Field security. They take the beer from his hand.

"He's underage," explains an "E" when the friend and security detail leave.

Ten minutes later, "D" returns to his seat.

"Did you get a ticket?" someone yells out.

"Nope," says "D," grinning widely.

The bleacher crowd responds with applause.

"Atta boy, buddy!"

It's the hottest day of the year to date and everyone in the bleachers is either shirtless or has their sleeves rolled up. A kid in front of us has one of those water bottle/fan contraptions and every so often he shows pity by spraying us.

Looking at the pitching matchup, it might be another loss for the Cubs. Toronto has Roy Halladay, the 2003 Cy Young winner, taking the mound. He has given up two earned runs in the previous thirty-eight innings for a 0.46 earned-run average. The Cubs have Sergio Mitre, an unproven right-hander who took Mark Prior's place in the rotation.

But straight from the files of "on any given day," Mitre pitches seven innings of scoreless ball, and even drives in a run with a double down the third base line in the third inning. The Cubs win 2–0, stopping Toronto's chances of a sweep.

Outside, everyone is already gearing up for the arrival of Red Sox Nation. The souvenir stands are selling "Red Sox Vs. Cubs" hats for twenty bucks apiece.

"I saw the Barnum and Bailey trucks pulling up out front," Cubs closer Ryan Dempster tells the media after the win. "It's going to be pretty nuts; that's for sure."

June 10–12—vs. Boston

Back in 2003, while the Cubs were busy frittering away a 3–1 NLCS lead to Florida, a similar thing was happening to the Boston Red Sox. Armed with a three-run lead in the eighth inning of game seven of the ALCS, Pedro Martinez and the Red Sox let the Yankees back into the game. And when Aaron Boone hit his home run in the bottom of the eleventh, a dream World Series matchup between the *Sawx* and Cubs had suddenly morphed into a laughable sports tragedy—Yankees versus Marlins.

What followed over the next few months was ludicrous, or at

least it was to me: The national media decided that the Red Sox were just like the Cubs!

So there were some similarities. Neither team had won a title since before Prohibition (Cubs—1908, Red Sox—1918). Both partially blamed curses (Billy Goat, Babe Ruth's ghost). Both had pinned down scapegoats (Bartman, Buckner).

But we still didn't appreciate being lumped in with those from Beantown. It all came down to the precise point of failure—would you rather die in a car accident at the base of Mount Everest or in an avalanche a thousand feet from the summit?

What I'm saying is that the main difference between the Cubs and Red Sox was—oh, how to put this delicately?—*the timing of being shit on.* Most years, the Cubs were done by the end of April. If they were lucky, they were done in by the June swoon. The Red Sox, meanwhile, became known for a laundry list of sobering late-season defeats—1949, '67, '75, '78, '86, '03.

While Bostonians bemoaned those late collapses, Cubs fans looked on and thought: "Ingrates! You may have been dumped, but at least you were still invited to the prom."

By the time the Red Sox made the ALCS in 2004, it was still hard for me to support them. But then Boston won games four and five after falling behind the Yankees three games to none. By game six, I was fully behind them. Who wouldn't support a late insurgency against Steinbrenner's Evil Empire?

After two more wins, the Red Sox ended up back in the World Series. When they actually won, I felt happy for them. For a *Star* assignment, I called Murphy's and the Cubby Bear. The managers there said that yes, Wrigleyville was happy for the Red Sox too. That Boston swept the Cardinals couldn't have hurt.

My happiness for Boston lasted about a week. Those from Boston kept carrying on and on, as if they had put a man on Mars. Center fielder Johnny Damon became a bottom-feeding celebrity. Bill "Sports Guy" Simmons devoted his next 283 columns on ESPN.com to the championship. Author Stephen King released *Faithful*, a tedious book that extracted $25 from the pockets of souvenir-hungry New Englanders.

By the time Bravo announced that several players would appear on *Queer Eye for the Straight Guy*, I renounced my temporary fanship. To me, the Red Sox had become no better than the Yankees. They could take that bloated payroll and that East Coast condescension and they could shove it.

Jealous bridesmaid behavior? Perhaps. But why did the Red Sox have to get there first? Why wasn't it the Cubs?

This weekend we must deal with the belle of the ball, up close and personal. The Red Sox are visiting Wrigley for the first time in team history. It's true that the Red Sox played (and beat) the Cubs in the 1918 World Series, but as everyone is quickly pointing out, those games were played at old Comiskey Park, which boasted a larger seating capacity.

Tickets are predictably in short supply for Boston's debut. My friend Dan sold four tickets on Craigslist for $800 a pair back in March and all the rooftops have been snatched up by visitors from Boston. Just this week, I saw several postings from an anonymous woman (or man?) on Craigslist.

```
Will trade sexual services for six (6) tick-
ets to Friday's game. E-mail for details.
```

Interested (for the purposes of research, you know) I sent an e-mail.

```
I have six tickets to the game. What are the
details?
```

A response arrived a half hour later.

```
Please send seat locations and pic.
```

Concerned the poster didn't quite understand the fundamentals of prostitution (namely, one cannot dictate the attractiveness of customers), the next e-mail was an attempt to teach.

```
Do you have any idea of the high demand for
this series? As far as I'm concerned, I could
look like Don Zimmer and you'd still have to
sleep with me for six (6!) tickets that are
together! I have no pic. Do you want the
tickets or not?
```

I received no response.

Perhaps the e-mailer, identified as *sassyirishlass*, found six tickets. Or maybe she knows about the loophole I'm trying right now. On the morning of each game, a certain number of tickets are released through the box office. These come from the tickets that are returned by the players from each team, from club execs, big-time sponsors, and whoever else. A skeptic might suggest these are the tickets that didn't get sold through the Cubs' premium ticket service, but that has never been proven.

Regardless, if I'm going to achieve my goal of spending less than $100 total for these three games, the early-morning ticket release is going to play a part.

Ben, a friend of my roommate, is visiting from Omaha. When we arrive at Wrigley, the line for tickets stretches from the Clark and Addison entrance to the Harry statue near Sheffield.

Somehow I am still drunk. Last night, at Kincade's, we overdosed on ten-cent chicken wings and cheap beer pitchers before heading to Zella, a bar in Lincoln Park, for a University of Wisconsin alumni gathering. There, I drank several beers and pretended to remember people who said they knew me from

Sellery Hall. Later, I uncharacteristically told a girl that if she wasn't going to take her shirt off, she "may as well get lost." That earned a shove and several disapproving looks from her friends. At the end of the night, before climbing into a cab home, I pulled my shirt over my head, flexed my nonexistent muscles, and then waved the shirt around my head.

It was that kind of night.

Still, duty calls, and, at 7:32 a.m., I am asking the thoughts of those around me. The ticket line will start moving in twenty-eight minutes.

Like me, Chris Hay is a twenty-six-year-old writer who lives in Chicago and loves the Cubs. Unlike me, he grew up in the Bronx. His father, Roger, is a Cubs fan who kept his blue roots in the middle of Yankee Heaven.

"It's how I was raised," Chris says. "One of my first memories is watching the Cubs lose in game five [of the 1984 NLCS]. I remember being really upset."

After graduating from Brown, Chris moved to Chicago in 2001 and started feeding his mania for the Cubs. Whether his presence has been good for the Cubs is not debatable, he says. In 2004, he went to twenty-two Cubs games. The team was 4–18 in those games, including a dismal 0–6 record in games against St. Louis.

Chris cannot stay away. When out-of-town friends come to visit, he automatically takes them to Wrigley. Since tickets are now in high demand, he awakes early and heads to the park to stand in line. "Screw the scalpers," Hayes says. I like this guy.

Until last year, the early-morning line was a well-kept secret. But word leaks out and I can spot several scalpers standing in line with us now. To their credit, several of the Cubs' workers have also seen them and are trying to roust them out. A guy behind me says that scalpers will pay homeless people to hold a spot in line overnight.

Hayes introduces me to Dan, a friend from Boston making his first trip to Wrigleyville. When he approached the front of the park, he couldn't believe his eyes.

"I looked at that big red sign and it just started to compute. . . . This is a famous place," Dan says. "I'm standing in front of a famous place right now."

Since he is the first Bostonian I've met today, I ask Dan to share a Bostonian's view of the Cubs. Surely, they have not paid Chicago any attention since the big World Series win. Right?

Wrong. Dan's opinion later proves to be prevalent. Bostonians, he says, feel for the Cubs and want them to win—preferably soon. Over the next seventy-two hours, Red Sox fans tell me this again and again. Any thoughts of this series being vicious, especially considering that Boston fans seem like roaches (they're everywhere), fly out the window.

"You know, last year, the Cubs executed a classic Red Sox collapse," Dan says. "So much was expected of them and they just constantly failed to deliver. Chris would call me and he'd be fed up. He'd say, 'You guys go through this *every* year?'"

The line starts to move. Dan has great expectations for his day at Wrigley. ("I suspect it's the second best park in America," he says, intent on making a point about Fenway.) After about ten minutes, we reach the ticket window. Chris and Dan go in front of me and score a pair of bleachers. My window appearance draws a pair in the 500 level, upper deck. Not the best seats, true, but they're only $17 apiece.

At least we're in the park.

When we reach our seats, there's a buzz and excitement that hasn't been present at Wrigley all season. The White Sox series was exciting, but since the two teams have been playing eight years now, it has become a little routine.

Playing Boston seems *momentous*. At least the media says it is. This week's newspapers and broadcasts have been filled with comparisons between the two curse-ridden franchises, no matter if one recently ended their drought. The *New York Times* did a story that landed on page A1. On one of the Sheffield rooftops, the Miller Lite billboard has been changed to read "One curse down. One to go." Even Mom knows this isn't a regular series; she calls to see if I've actually gotten tickets to the game.

This is a big event and it feels like it. Maybe it was the ticket challenge or maybe it's the visit from the reigning World Champions . . . I don't know. The tingle rushes up through my arms and I turn to give my sister, Kristin—the lucky recipient of my extra ticket—a playful punch on the arm. She smiles. She's ready too.

We're surrounded by New Englanders in the stands. And every time I hear them talk—"You have a nice *pahk*"—I laugh. It seems as if the entire city of Boston moved west for the weekend.

The Cubs give the tourists a rude welcoming. Jeromy Burnitz belts a three-run home run in the second inning, followed by a two-run shot from Todd Hollandsworth. After a single run by Boston in the top of the inning, the Cubs score three runs in the bottom of the third to open an 8–1 lead over pitcher Bronson Arroyo and the Red Sox. By the time Greg Maddux hits a home run that catches the basket in left, we are delirious. The Cubs are on their way to a 14–6 series-opening win.

Though the weather is muggy, no one seems to mind. From our seats in the right field upper deck, we can see everything both inside and outside the park. When Burnitz hits another home run, this time over the right field fence, we see a man with a glove catch the ball on the fly.

In front of me sits Mary Rita, a fifty-one-year-old from Ludlow, Vermont. "A Red Sox fan?" I inquire. She stares at me. Her face says, "Are you kidding?"

Turns out that Mary Rita is a Cubs fan living in Red Sox Nation. She grew up in Oak Park and worked as an usher in 1969, the year of the collapse. Now she lives in Vermont and follows the team from afar. She even made the owner of her favorite bar subscribe to MLB Extra Innings so she could watch the games.

Sitting next to her friend Hank, Mary Rita asks me about my CUBS: BELIEVE bracelet. We start talking, but our conversation abruptly stops whenever she needs to record a play on her scorecard. (Kristin loves Mary Rita's devotion. "She's *soo* cute!" she says.)

Mary Rita and Hank have been making a trip to Wrigley every year for the past eighteen seasons. They need to get their "Chicago fix." The easiest way to do that? A pie from Uno's Pizza, of course.

"My first game was in 1962," Mary Rita says. "They played the Phillies. My dad always took us to games. We went to see all the teams. We had season tickets to the Blackhawks and we were there when Bobby Hull scored his fiftieth goal. I still remember getting doused by beer because we were sitting in the first row of the balcony."

Mary Rita came to Chicago with no tickets, but wasn't fazed. She knew she'd get in. We hadn't seen them, but Mary Rita and Hank were sitting in line this morning.

"You know, I haven't lived in Chicago full-time since I was eighteen years old," she says. "But I still call this my home. If anyone asks where I'm from, it's an easy response. I'm from Chicago."

Saturday, June 11—vs. Boston

With the knowledge of the early-morning ticket line, I feel like the secrets to ticket world have opened up. It's not as fun as wrangling and sparring with the scalpers, but with thousands of Red Sox fans driving up prices, what choice do I have?

For the second day in a row, Ben and I wake early and head to the park. Again we are battling the cobwebs in our heads; a rough night at Bluesfest in Grant Park will do that.

We stand/sit in line for two hours, weathering a visit from Ronnie Woo just after eight a.m. Several people in line hand Ronnie their cell phones so he can give wake-up calls to those still asleep.

Wake up! Woo! Cubs! Woo! World! Woo! Series! Woo!

Since we're actually farther back than yesterday, we ponder our chances for tickets. When the line starts moving, it becomes a tense waiting game. Can we get to the window before all the tickets are gone?

Nope. We're about fifty people away when the windows shutter and everyone starts yelling, "Sold out! Sold out!" A guy who just bought $17 tickets comes by, eyes my University of Iowa T-shirt, and offers them to me.

"Because you're a Hawkeye, a hundred dollars apiece."

How collegial of him.

I decline, and so the game is on. At one p.m., Dan, my college editor, meets me on Sheffield for a full-scale battle of Screw the Scalper. In the first ten minutes, we see the market has dropped a little bit—no one's paying $150 a ticket—but most tickets are still going for twice the face value.

A man and his wife offer us two terrace reserved tickets for $95 apiece. Within two minutes, the haggling goes hard-core—the man wants $50, but we are offering $40. The wife starts balking—"But we paid $150 apiece for them!" We laugh. It is not our fault that these two were swept up in such bravado over the Boston series. "It's a buyer's market," we tell them with just a bit of bullshit. It's forty dollars for a ticket or we're walking.

The man grimaces. Dan shoots a look at me. *Hold your ground. Don't agree to fifty. Everything will be fine. We're getting into this game.* The man agrees while the wife sighs. We are victorious.

We've paid two dollars over face. We peel off four twenties and hand them over.

"See you inside," says the man, clearly not in a good mood.

Reality sinks in. Unlike buying from a scalper, we now have to sit with a man we just emasculated in front of his wife. For an entire game. Almost three hours. At this point, I start to think we should have paid $50.

Not Dan. When filleting a guy with extras, he can be a cold, remorseless dude. "We got our price," he says.

We take our seats and the man makes a snide remark I can't quite make out. It seems like this might be a long game, so I resort to the best option at a time like this.

"Hey, let me buy you guys a beer," I offer.

And suddenly it's like that old ad jingle: *Buy that man a Miller beer! The best comes shining through!* Even though they don't sell Miller in Wrigley, Michael is now my best friend. His frown has disappeared.

"That'd be great," he says.

"Next time the vendor comes around," I promise.

Beth, Michael's wife, is not as easily swayed. Eventually, though, she comes around. With three Old Styles now being shared by combat veterans, I ask Michael to analyze our bargaining skills.

Were we too pushy? Did we come off as assholes?

It's unclear what answer I'm looking for. Being a pushy asshole probably worked in our favor. But Michael and Beth are nice enough people, do we really want such a label?

"You guys just did a great job," Michael says. "We were at Murphy's before and a scalper offered us $150 a ticket, but we figured the price was only going to go up, so we told him no.

"I didn't know that a lot of people were going to be selling out on the street. After hanging out there and getting no bites, I just wanted to get into the game. I don't blame you. I blame myself."

The Red Sox take an early 3–0 lead when Zambrano walks two in the first inning, then gives up a three-run homer to Trot Nixon. Bill Mueller makes it 4–0 with a dinger in the second, and it looks like we're in for a long day. Zambrano just simply doesn't have it. Maybe we can take two of three by winning tomorrow's game—a Sunday nighter on ESPN.

But, wait . . . what's this? The Cubs score three runs in the bottom of the second. An RBI groundout by Hollandsworth ties the game in the bottom of the third.

Michael shares his story. He grew up in Maryland and went to "only three Orioles games between the ages of one and twenty-five." A graduate of Notre Dame, he moved to Chicago in 1998. He had no roommates, didn't know anybody and was generally miserable.

On July 24, 1998, he and an out-of-town friend went to Wrigley for a doubleheader with the New York Mets. After two Cubs losses, Michael headed to Sports Corner. They staked out a table, ordered a few beers, and talked about Michael's new life in Chicago. After a while a woman and her friends walked through the door. Michael glanced at her.

It was Beth.

Beth, a Buffalo Grove native, was wild about the Cubs. They started dating, and Michael was soon a serious Cubs convert. Four years later, Michael gave her a blindfold and put Beth inside a car. When they arrived at their destination, she was standing at home plate, in an empty Wrigley Field. Michael was holding a ring.

"Everyone wants to propose during the game," Michael says. "But nobody wants to do it when the stadium's empty. That's how we got in. Now we're happily married."

"For now," says Beth, as Michael again leans over to flirt with a lithe twenty-two-year-old to the right of us.

The Cubs complete their comeback by taking a 5–4 lead. In

the bottom of the eighth, they go ahead 7–4. Ryan Dempster enters in the ninth to save the game. He immediately gives up two runs. Everyone stands with Manny Ramirez on second base and Trot Nixon, the tying run, coming to the plate.

With butterflies racing through my stomach, I turn to Dan.

"I can't take this."

"It's the Cubs. You know this is how it goes."

On the next pitch, Nixon pops out to Aramis Ramirez for the final out. The Cubs' portion of the stadium erupts. Party time.

The Cubs go for the sweep on Sunday night, live on ESPN's national game of the week. I squeeze into a seat in the last row of the upper deck, on the right field side of the press box. The last game turned out to be the toughest, and I had to pay $30, thirteen over face for the privilege. (Sacrilege!)

Three straight games over the Carmines isn't happening. Boston takes an 8–1 victory, and after the game, the city of Chicago exhales. We survived the invasion. In the next day's *Boston Globe*, a fan describes the weekend as a meeting between the "biggest losers in history."

Perhaps. But we will gladly switch places with the Red Sox anytime. The accents? They can keep them.

Chapter Nine

Algonquin for "the Good Land"

One day, when I was seven years old, Dad came home with some news: We were going to a White Sox game.

This in itself was not news. Back then, we went to six or seven games a year. Each time, I'd eat one or two hot dogs, my dad would buy me a pennant, we'd watch the Sox win or lose, and then we'd go home. It was routine.

This trip, however, would be different.

"We're going to the game on a bus," said Dad.

For someone who was driven to school, riding on a bus was an *event*.

Later that week, we set off on an ordinary yellow school bus— "we" meaning me, my father, and about forty members from a veterans' club on the southeast side of Chicago.

From the last row of the bus, I watched as each club member climbed aboard. They were working-class guys; most had long beards and well-developed beer bellies. A majority had served in Vietnam. They worked during the day, then spent most of their free time hanging out at "The Post" in Burnham, where member dues allowed for twenty-five-cent Lite taps and free popcorn from the old machine in the corner.

It soon became apparent, probably even to a seven-year-old, that the trip to Comiskey was just a way to mobilize their over-consumption. Two members rolled a keg down the aisle, then stood it upright and tapped it like they were astronauts planting the flag on the moon. The guys to the left of us had pocket flasks. So did the ones in front of us. I could smell the whiskey on their breath when they turned to talk to the skinny kid (me) who was toting his baseball glove. They watched their cussing, or at least while they remembered I was there. They called me "Ken's son."

On the trip home, the guy in front of us kept leaning over his seat and thrusting a small jar into my face. "Wanna herring, young man?" he asked.

I pretended to gag, then shook my head while trying to keep a close eye on the jar's terrifying contents.

A herring? For a seven-year-old?

"Don't know what you're missing, little brutha!" he said before pinching his fingers around the slime and dropping it in his mouth.

He repeated this action (and the "don't know what you're missing" bit) five or six times on the ride home. To this day, I have never met another person who carried herring for postdrink snacking. Or, for that matter, carried herring for post-*anything* snacking.

Dad, for his part, did a good job in protecting me that night. He was not a Vietnam vet nor a big drinker, and his facial hair (a sweet Fu Manchu) had been gone since his early twenties.

Some of Mom's cousins, members of the club who invited us along, were all of these things. The trip, I suspect, was simply for my benefit. Dad knew I loved baseball and tried to take me to as many games as possible. When thrown into that situation aboard the boozy bus, he looked straight ahead and probably said a silent prayer that Mom wouldn't find out. To my knowledge, she never did.

I tell this story not to illustrate a scarring youthful experience, but instead to detail the genesis of my love for bus trips. While that bus may have been no place for a child, and no doubt Dad realized this five seconds after boarding, I didn't mind. Looking past the drinking (which was most likely a problem for most of those guys), one saw a group of friends, confined in close, jostling quarters. They laughed. They joked. They *bullshitted*. The bus trip represented a night out, away from life's usual norms and toward a temporary feeling of an even bigger community at Thirty-fifth and Shields. That feeling, I realized years later, stuck with me.

Since that trip, I have ridden buses with the Boy Scouts, my friend's church, and my sixth-grade class to Wrigley for a Cubs game. As a sophomore at the University of Wisconsin, I made the eight-hour trip to Ann Arbor on a chartered bus for the Badger-Wolverine game. We were raving drunk by the time we reached the Illiana border, the result of drinking Bacardi poured into a half-empty two-liter bottle of Coca-Cola. When we hit Valparaiso, we bought a warm case of Bud Light and drank that.

Today I'm headed to Milwaukee for the third game in a four-game series with the Brew Crew. Our mode of transportation is a Chicago Charter bus that is painted with a silhouette of the city's skyline. We are leaving from the corner of Waveland and Sheffield, just outside the entrance to the bleachers.

Let me explain how I got here. About a week ago, I was browsing the Internet, doing nothing in particular, when an ad jumped out from the Web site of theheckler.com: "SEE THE CUBS IN MILWAUKEE FOR JUST $55!"

Upon further inspection, the money was good for:

- a chartered bus trip to/from Milwaukee
- a ticket to the game

- a cookout in the Miller Park parking lot (Drumroll, please)
- all the beer one can humanly drink, before and after the game.

Actually, the advertisement wasn't clear about beer being provided. So I e-mailed Laura, the trip coordinator, and asked if we could bring "refreshments" on the bus. "Your ticket price includes beer," she e-mailed back. "Did you have something else in mind?"

I probably should have just said "beer" instead of being coy and using "refreshments." Yet it took restraint not to e-mail her back with some paraphrased Hunter S. Thompson lines:

"Well, Laura, we need to make this bus look like a mobile police narcotics lab. . . . Not that we need it all for the trip, but once you get locked into a serious drug collection, the tendency is to push it as far as you can."

Instead, I replied, lamely, *"Beer on a bus! What a novel idea!"*

By game day, a Wednesday, I have recruited Art and his fiancée, Angie, along for the trip. Art is a schoolteacher and spends his summers charting O'Hare flight patterns from his backyard. Angie works in retail and has an odd schedule. She has enlisted a few other trip-goers; all of them are playing hooky.

Upon arriving at Wrigley, we see what we're dealing with. There are few people our age—a couple of overaged fratboys from the trendy Bucktown neighborhood, a group of gun-shy thirty-something girls from Ravenswood. Some are writers for the *Heckler*, an on-point Cubs-centric version of the *Onion*. Others are people I recognize from around the park. In particular there is one man in his fifties who wears a hard-plastic, safari-style Cubs hat, and cheap sunglasses he probably bought at Walgreens.

Until today, I thought this man was blind. After each home

game, he stands at the corner of Clark and Addison. He carries a canvas bag filled with stuffed toy goats and blue-and-red beads. Because he never moves from that spot and because he wears those silly sunglasses and hat, it's easy to think his eyes don't work.

He has to be the worst street vendor I've ever seen. He is timid and doesn't make much noise. His sales pitch goes like this: *"Guhhh-oats! . . . Guhh-oats! . . . Get your guhh-oats! . . . I got guhh-oats here!"* I have never seen him make a sale. He has brought his bag of goats along for the trip. Perhaps he thinks he will sell some in Milwaukee.

Ronnie Woo is here, too. Like that morning of the Boston game, someone hands him a cell phone and instructs him to leave a message from a friend. When he comes by our party, I snap my first-ever picture with him.

Later, he boards the bus but quickly leaves.

"They don't allow black people in Wisconsin," Art deadpans.

If you've ever been to Green Bay, where every black man is assumed to play for the Packers, you know Art is only half kidding.

Beerific. That's Milwaukee in one terribly made-up word. The City That Breweries Built is only a ninety-mile trip up the Lake Michigan coast, so there's never an excuse not to make a run to the Cheese State. When Dad was an underage kid in college, they'd hit the Wrigley bleachers in the afternoon and then head to County Stadium at night, where the staff looked at their Cubs ticket stubs and let them in. Since the drinking age was then eighteen in Wisconsin, Dad and his friends could drink. He swears that County Stadium used to sell beer in a bucket. I only sort of believe him.

To get to Milwaukee, take the Edens Expressway to I-94 North, past the affluent North Shore suburbs and past the roller coasters at Six Flags Great America in Gurnee. Pay the toll that pisses off each Wisconsinite and enter through Kenosha, home to several outlet malls. Pass the sign for "Bong Recreation Area." Make the ten millionth marijuana-related wisecrack. (Fact: Richard Bong was actually America's ace fighter pilot in World War II.) Fight a losing battle to stop the bus at the cholesterol-threatening Mars Cheese Castle and the Bobby Nelson Sausage Shop. Hightail it through Racine, then enter Milwaukee, head west on I-894 and gawk when approaching Miller Park, the $400 million retractable-roof stadium that opened in 2001, home of the Milwaukee Brewers.

The residents of Illinois and Wisconsin have always had a love-hate relationship. And by that I mean Illinois natives love Wisconsin, while the fine people from Wisconsin *hate* Illinois.

We look at Wisconsin and see a natural paradise, a place to drive on weekends while towing our boats behind our SUVs with the Land of Lincoln plates. We see tourist traps like the Dells and Door County, where we can let our mothers and grandmothers roam free, purchasing things like moccasins, saltwater taffy, and homemade fudge. We see the University of Wisconsin, one of the country's finest public schools, where snotty North Shore girls can join sororities before backstabbing genuinely nice girls from places like Prairie du Chien and Eau Claire.

In short, we wouldn't mind annexing the entire place.

Wisconsin hates us, well, for all of the above reasons. They also say we drive too fast, charge too many tolls, and don't have enough common sense to root for America's team (so they say), the Green Bay Packers. They call us names like F.I.B.'s (Fucking Illinois Bastards) and F.I.S.H. (Fucking Illinois Shitheads). A typical joke: *What's the difference between a Cheesehead and a dickhead? The Wisconsin-Illinois state line.*

We get our revenge. The bus pulls up to Miller Park and we F.I.B.'s pile out. (Art has already downed, by my count, eight beers.) On the parking lot's horizon is an armada of charter buses, all lined up like tanks from an invading army. Each is packed with Cubs fans.

Miller Park has become Wrigley Field North, and for good reason. Because tickets at Wrigley sold so quickly in February, many churches, schools, and Scout groups were shut out. As an alternative, they rented buses and headed to Milwaukee.

"We have arrived!" yells Art, planting his right foot on the top of a cooler, Captain Morgan style. And so we have.

Brewers' pregame is much different from the celebrations in Wrigleyville. When the plans for Miller Park were being debated, one group pushed for a downtown location. But that would have meant limited tailgate opportunities, which are largely considered a Wisconsin birthright. Ultimately the stadium was built in the center field parking lot of County Stadium, which was located just off a freeway and is surrounded by parking lots full of guys drinking from cases of Miller Lite. Everyone huddles around Smokey Joe grills.

Tailgating—now here's my element. Once, at the *Star*, my editor assigned me to a story at a Chiefs playoff game. My task was to roam the Arrowhead parking lot before the game, aiming to eat as much as possible. Ribs. Jambalaya. Chicken wings. Chili made with moose meat. The story almost ended with me throwing up on ESPN's John Clayton as he passed in the press box.

One essential truth stuck from that assignment. If you are ever hungry at a game and have no food, buy a seventy-nine-cent notepad and start roaming. If tailgaters believe you are writing an article about them (it doesn't hurt to have a photographer at your side), people will give you whatever you want.

Because the *Heckler* trip is offering only grilled hot dogs, I set out on a mission. There's little rhyme or reason to the first two tailgates I select. At one, an inebriated man wearing a Mark Grace jersey tells me that no one's in charge and I cannot speak to anyone about the barbecue. I start making a cheeseburger from the tailgate's spread and wait to see if he or anyone else protests. No one does.

At the bus next door, I talk to a man named John who is with a group from Bolingbrook. With cheeseburger still in my mouth, I point to his pot of Italian sausage and raise my eyebrows.

"You want some peppers or red sauce on it?" he asks.

Jackpot.

After ten minutes with John, it's time to address a group with a yellow school bus. "I'm looking for a good bratwurst," I announce.

"We've got an extra one right here," says George Richardson.

Before long, I am talking with George and his wife, Wendy. They own a farm in Spring Grove, Illinois, just miles from the Wisconsin border. Wendy says I should come up sometime—they own the largest corn maze in Illinois. This year's theme is the twentieth anniversary of the 1985 Chicago Bears Super Bowl team. They've worked out endorsements and everything. Because I have been drinking, I tell Wendy that yes, it is entirely possible I will drive an hour to come check out her corn maze.

"It's really tough to get through," she says.

"What's with this trip to Miller Park?" I ask.

"We do this through the Rotary Club in Richmond," George explains. "We hold an auction every year in April that raises money for different things, like high school scholarships. This year we raised over eleven thousand dollars. This trip is always our reward for that hard work.

"We've got about forty or forty-five people on this bus. They each paid twenty-five dollars. We used to come up for the White Sox–Brewers games, but when they switched to the National League we changed over to the Cubs series. We couldn't get group tickets at Wrigley if we tried. Plus, there's nowhere to tailgate around there.

"Am I a big Cubs fan? I'm a bigger fan when they're winning. But it's fun to come out here either way."

George looks and sounds like he's in charge of this whole trip. But he's not. Marty Martinson is the man, George says.

Marty walks over and shakes my hand. Is he responsible for this interstate caravan? And why didn't they rent a bus with an onboard bathroom?

"I just buy the bratwurst," Marty says.

"It's good bratwurst," I tell him.

On the walk to the stadium, a few more Brewers shirts become visible. Still, Cubs fans outnumber the supporters from the home team. Chicago has taken the first two games in this series, behind good pitching performances from Greg Maddux (who tied Tom Seaver with his 311th career victory on Monday) and Jerome Williams, a stocky puka-shell-necklace-wearing call-up from Iowa. The wins were a nice elixir for the Cubs, who were swept in last weekend's visit to Yankee Stadium, the team's first since 1938.

A win against the Brewers tonight might come easy. Zambrano is on the hill and we feel reasonably confident. The Brewers, after an early surge to second place in the NL Central, are back where they belong—under .500.

Of course, this does not happen. Zambrano implodes in the second inning, giving up eight runs for a buzz-beating deficit. Worse yet, our seats are *above* Bernie Brewer's Chalet, so when he slides down after a Brewer home run, we are actually looking down at the suds-craving mascot.

The Cubs eventually lose 9–4 (and 8–7 on Thursday), but we make the trip worthwhile. After the second-inning surge, we head downstairs, where, for $5.75, I buy perhaps the best treat in the majors—cheese fries in a plastic Brewers helmet.

We situate ourselves at a table in the middle of the concourse, which is right next to the condiments table. Next to the onions and relish are three spigots marked "Ketchup," "Mustard" and "Secret Sauce." I am eating a pretzel. Art is throwing back $6 bottles of Miller Lite like they're free.

Angie is trying to eat all of my cheese fries.

"Artie, you could offer me mind-blowing sex or these cheese fries and I'd choose the cheese fries," she says. "You know what this is?"

Do we want to know?

"It's an orgasm in a helmet," Angie loudly announces.

Apparently not.

After pondering a creature with cheddar ejaculate (if one existed, no doubt we'd find it in Wisconsin), we sneak down into the best seats in the house, ten rows off home plate. Miller Park does not have Wrigley's crotchety, seat-guarding ushers. These are the best seats I'll have all year.

When we get back on the bus, an interloper joins us.

"Is this bus going back to Chicago?" asks the twenty-something male, who is wearing a Cubs hat with mesh backing and a Sigma Pi "2003 Rush" T-shirt.

When someone says yes, the erstwhile and obviously obliterated frattie takes a seat and immediately passes out for the remainder of the trip. His cell phone keeps buzzing—his friends wondering where he's gone.

The bus hits Kenosha and I have a sudden urge for a jar of herring.

Chapter Ten

Pearls from the Sky

Tuesday, June 28—vs. Milwaukee

The plan had been to observe the first day, participate the second.

But damned if I don't want this baseball. As soon as I pick up the ball's trajectory, it starts to descend. It's definitely coming onto Waveland, and a prescient group has clustered between the crosswalk lines on Kenmore. No baseballs have come close to me today, and this one doesn't seem any different. I know the drill—Ken Vangeloff is going to catch the ball on a fly.

But then, a serendipitous turn. Several kids crash into Vangeloff and the ball—hit from the bat of Milwaukee's Carlos Lee—collides with the pavement. I am standing a few feet behind the scrum and the ball bounces over my head. If I play this right, I'm going home with a baseball.

I turn down Kenmore and sprint a couple of steps. The ball bounces again, about seven feet in the air, then again at about five. I make a flashing grab with my left hand, which is bare, and pull it back—it is empty.

The crowd catches up to me and the ball bounces again. It feels like I'm in the middle of uncontrolled violence, like how a fight will often tumble down from a bar's steps and into the middle of the street. There's no rhyme or reason. Everyone is scrambling.

There! It's right in front of me. My arm flashes again and—cripes—I would have had it if my glove was here. I grabbed too fast. Someone's arms are around my waist and I fall to a knee. There is a tussle in front of me, and then a kid with a cutoff Chicago Bulls shirt thrusts his right hand in the air.

He is holding the baseball.

Damn!

I hate that kid.

It's three months into the season and I've met some interesting people. But there are few more fascinating, I think, than the guys who come out, day after day, to chase baseballs on Waveland Avenue.

If one were to imagine a being whose sole purpose on Earth is to chase baseballs, one might assume the subject would look like this: a young boy, perhaps in his teens, maybe a couple years older, quick of foot and aggressive to a fault. He carries a glove, has the latest Nike shoes, wears Bolle sunglasses and a backward Cubs hat.

The description would be wrong. The self-titled "Ballhawks" look nothing like this when they set up shop on Waveland. There are six or seven who act as perpetual Rawlings stalkers, though the number varies from season to season.

Most of the guys are past thirty. They wear Canseco-style Oakleys, sweat shorts, and knee braces. Their appearances, however, are deceiving. When a ball is hit, they're the first ones to track it, the first ones to make a move. Most of the time, they're catching the ball in the air while everyone is still deciding what to do.

It'd be clichéd to say these guys used to "toil in anonymity," but that's more or less the truth. Then came the Sammy–Big Mac battle in '98, and their cachet increased. *Oh, the gift and the curse.* With newfound fame came more Ballhawks-for-a-day. When Sosa hit his sixty-second, the godfather of Ballhawks, Moe Mullins, actually landed on the pearl in the alley to the east of the Budweiser building. In the ensuing pile, Mullins had his thumb pulled back and the ball came loose. Mullins, who has been coming out to the park since 1958, filed a lawsuit to regain possession of the ball. He withdrew it weeks later. He still doesn't have the ball. Don't cry for him, though: He's got over forty-five hundred at home.

Milwaukee is back in town for a three-game series, the Brew Crew's last visit for the year. I'm tired of watching the Brewers. Yeah, they're an NL Central rival and everything, but apart from Carlos Lee, no one on the team does anything for me. Besides, I still find it strange that they're in the National League. Give me Robin Yount and Paul Molitor from the Brewers' American League days. Then we'd be talking.

In lieu of heading inside the ballpark, I am opting for a three-game vacation with the Ballhawks. It's true. I'm going to look stupid, twenty-six years old and wearing a baseball glove in the middle of a public street. People might snicker behind my back. They might laugh at my face. But if I have learned anything by watching the Ballhawks, it is this: For most people, catching a baseball at a major league game is a cataclysmic meeting of fates, an opening of the heavens, a smile from the baseball gods.

For the Ballhawks, catching a baseball is only a matter of time. Simple math. Eliminate chance. That's how they do it. Take x number of balls that clear the left field fence during games and batting practice, multiply it by 81 home dates, and subtract a few for the days when the wind is blowing fiercely out or player hangovers cancel B.P. The end result is a baseball pie that gets divided by the dedicated few and, regrettably for the Ballhawks, also by some lucky bystanders.

Vangeloff, a forty-something accountant who works from home, is the first one to give me a few pointers. Because his designated spot is in the crosswalk, he's often the first to be pestered by questions. Today, I'm the questioner.

He doesn't mind if people observe as long as they don't get in his way. I position myself a few feet behind him, and Vangeloff gets into his game stance. It's not that intense. His arms are crossed over his soft lower stomach, a glove on his right hand. He wears a Tigers hat and wraparound sunglasses. His eyes are looking toward the sky. He is pivoting on the balls of his feet.

Occasionally, Vangeloff will make a move toward the wall, in anticipation of a street-bound ball. A lot of times, though, it's a false alarm, and the ball falls into the bleachers as a gift for early-arriving fans.

My questions start coming. How does he see the ball so quickly? After all, we can't see the batter from where we're standing. We can't see any of the game.

"See how we can see the roof of the stadium?" he asks.

I do. The roof's façade is green and narrow.

"Well, the baseball stands out against it when it's hit. We can track it against the front of the press box, too. From there, it's a matter of whether it's coming out or not.

"Today is a bad sky day. See how it's not blue, but it's not gray? It's kind of hazy and it's tough to pick the ball out. We like the days when it's really blue out."

A few cars pass by on Waveland. Both sides of the street have been blocked off, but residents can still sneak by. Large buses also make their way through, dropping off loads of groups from places like Davenport, Iowa. Add to that a constant stream of fans and workers coming home from the El, and you've got quite a commotion.

I'm still asking questions when a ball comes flying into the street. It's too far away for Vangeloff to have a chance, but there's a good crowd chasing after it. Out of the corner of my eye I see a FedEx truck flying down the road. The focused crowd running into the middle of the street doesn't notice it.

In the face of catastrophe, several thoughts run through my mind:

Holy shit, I'm about to see someone get killed by a FedEx truck! This is going to be sad. But also great for the book.

The sidewalk inhabitants are frozen, waiting to see what happens. There's a screeching of brakes and then some skidding. I see the driver through the windshield. His eyes are wide, his teeth are clenched and he's gripping the wheel. You know that he's thinking about taking a different route next time, if only God—or physics—lets him out of this one.

The bulky truck lurches forward and then . . . miraculously stops. Someone's packages in the back must be broken, but no one is hurt outside. The driver lets out a sigh of relief and somehow laughs a few seconds later. A Ballhawk-for-a-day comes away with the ball. No one in the chasing group seems to notice how close they came to getting smacked by several tons of next-day delivery.

"How many people have you seen been hit by cars?"

"None," says Vangeloff, who didn't participate in the fray and barely took his eyes off the sky to watch.

"Seriously? You've never seen it?"

"Not yet," he says.

Vangeloff's story reads like this: He moved to Chicago in 1990 and started attending Cubs games almost immediately.

After a few games in the bleachers, Vangeloff looked toward Waveland. "I wondered where the balls went after they cleared the fence," he says. Over the next few weeks, he came out to Waveland and chased baseballs. He saved money by not going into the game. By mid-season, when the All-Star Game hit Wrigley, he was a full-fledged Ballhawk.

"Been here ever since," he says.

Vangeloff runs a Web site—www.ballhawk.com, which details each ball hit out of the park. His interests are simply baseball. If you were to make a list of his favorite teams, he says, it would read Pirates, Cubs, Indians, and whoever's playing the Yankees. Each year, he buys a new baseball hat—the cap of the worst team that year. He figures that team could use the merchandise revenue. His Detroit hat is the product of a 55–106 season in 2002.

In midquestion, Vangeloff bolts across the street. He bumps into an older woman while attempting to position himself under a fence-clearing ball. The ball grazes the woman, and then hits the ground. Vangeloff picks it up, then hands it to the woman, who looks confused.

When he returns from across the street, another Ballhawk looks equally confused. "Why'd you give her that? Was she crying?"

"Nah," says Vangeloff. "But it hit her. It's the right thing to do."

The Ballhawks line up like sentries along Waveland. Vangeloff's spot is in the crosswalk. Rich Buhrke, who has been out here almost as long as Moe, stands in front of the yellow building to Vangeloff's right. When left-handers come to the plate, Buhrke hurries to the right field fence on Sheffield.

Andy Mielke prowls in front of the Budweiser building. If someone hits a power-alley blast, it's his. Dave Davison is the freelancer in the group; he stands in front of Vangeloff but drifts around. Moe calls him the best Ballhawk in the game today.

Moe takes batting practice in the bleachers, in left field, where the fence drops to a shorter level. Occasionally he turns around to tell his friends if there's a lefty or righty at the plate. When B.P. is finished, Mullins comes back out onto the street.

"Does Moe actually buy a ticket just for batting practice?" I ask Mielke.

Mielke shakes his head. "I know how he gets in. And I can tell you if you promise not to put it in your book."

"I'll just ask Moe."

"Yeah, but he won't tell you either."

By now, I have deduced that Moe does not pay to go inside.

Mielke starts citing statistics to me. Like Mullins and Buhrke, he has caught over four thousand balls. Davison is in that neighborhood as well. Vangeloff has a modest twenty-five hundred. They keep all the game-hit home runs. They keep some of the other baseballs in tubs and boxes around the house. Some they donate to Little Leagues. Others they give away to friends.

This year might be their last hurrah. When the Wrigley expansion takes place this winter, the Ballhawks will be severely affected. Almost eighteen hundred seats are being added to the bleachers, so the outer wall will be moved closer to the sidewalk. The stands and fences will be higher, so fewer balls will come out. When one does, the ball's flight won't be easily trackable. It'll be like standing underneath a coconut tree while wearing a blindfold.

Most of the guys say they plan to come out next year. They just need to see how high the added rows of bleachers will be. Still, the situation seems hopeless.

"Most of these guys are upset about the expansion," says Mielke, a thirty-eight-year-old salesman who's been coming out since 1978, the year I was born. "But not me. I'm looking forward to finally playing some more golf."

This is a curious admission. To hear Mielke talk, it's like he has been held by an obsession for twenty-seven years. Not coming to the park is not in his free will. As long as there are baseballs flying out of the park, Mielke needs to be here. He has no choice in the matter.

Mielke's actions back this belief. Though you wouldn't mind having a beer with him afterward, you wouldn't want to butt heads with him over a baseball.

He is intense. He is serious. The glove on his left hand costs $250. It's the same model used by Barry Bonds, Mielke's favorite player. When Mielke secures a ball—which is often—there's little time for celebration. The routine goes like this: Catch ball. Take ball from glove. Shove it in pocket. Return to stance. Look for next ball.

Mielke tells me that he caught three of the record twenty home runs that Sosa hit in June of 1998. He has the first home run in Devil Ray history, a blast from Bubba Trammell at Tropicana Field. He attends spring training each year with the sole intent of collecting more baseballs.

By now the game has started, and I am just recovering from not grabbing that loose ball. Mielke keeps saying he wants to leave and go do some laundry at his house, which is near Addison and Ashland. Perhaps predictably, he is still at Wrigley.

His cell rings. He swears, then fishes into his pocket.

"Who the hell is calling me when Derrek Lee is up?"

He glances at the caller ID.

"It's my girlfriend. She can wait."

June 29

I wake up around eight, make some eggs and read the game stories in the *Tribune* and *Sun-Times*. Combined with two weekend wins against the Sox at the Cell, the Cubs have extended their winning streak to three. Last night's win looked like a momentum builder. Zambrano pitched a 2–0 shutout. Patterson made a can-you-believe-that catch to kill a rally in the eighth, which drew large cheers. Then he led off the bottom of the inning with a strikeout, which drew boos. With Hawkins now gone, Patterson is the new whipping boy for Cubs fans.

Apart from the *Sports Center* highlights, I didn't see the game. I was on Waveland. No game balls came over the fence. There was little to do except talk to the Ballhawks, watch girls walk by, and listen to Pat and Ron via my Wal-Mart headset. At the end of the night, I asked Rich Buhrke, the veteran, if he considered it a waste of time if no home runs reached the street during a game.

"Not really," he said.

I have plans to meet Vangeloff at Waveland and Kenmore at 10:45 a.m. I leave my apartment with a notepad, my headphones, two bottles of frozen water, and, most important, my Rawlings glove, a left-handed model signed strangely by righty Robin Yount. The mitt is over fifteen years old and it's been everywhere I've ever lived. Bartlett, Madison, Kansas City, and now, Chicago. My childhood phone number is written in sixth-grade Sharpie on the back. If it gets lost they can still call it and send it back to my parents.

This glove shall be my salvation.

When I reach the intersection, Vangeloff is nowhere to be found. Instead, there are two younger members of the crew—Mark Loiacano, an Anthony Kiedis look-alike who is wearing camouflage pants and no shirt, and George Field, a forty-three-year-old Latino who looks twenty years younger. His most visible feature is a shark tattoo on his neck. Don't laugh—both of them are pulling off their looks.

"The Cubs have been known not to hit after a night game," says Mark, who has a long pile of hair underneath his blue Cubs hat.

This is the classic Ballhawk bellyaching, which is perhaps the only skill the group has perfected more than the baseball chase. Later, Davison will contend that this year's team is the worst batting-practice squad he's ever seen.

"They don't have a lot of home run hitters," Davison explains.

"And the couple they do have are trying to raise their averages. Derrek Lee is almost at .400, so he's picking his pitches and trying to place the ball all over the field. Nothing ever comes out here. Everything we're going to get today is going to come from Milwaukee."

I set down my bottles of water by the corner fire hydrant and start to wait. Mark has a story about catching Sosa's 514th career home run, hit on July 9, 2003, two home runs after surpassing Ernie Banks's career total of 512. To hear him tell it, he evaded dozens of other hawks, a parked cab, the fire hydrant, a moving cab, and several scratches before running it down on Kenmore and suffering a concussion. It is Mark's trophy trout, the one he keeps separate from all others, the one he brags about, the one he tells stories about.

This is why I—and most other people—do not come out here every day. To me, Sosa's home run ball would look like all the others Mark has caught over the past two years. Each weighs five ounces, costs around thirteen bucks, and bears the signature of "Allen H. Selig—Commissioner." Nothing distinguishes one ball from the other. I can appreciate the story behind Mark's ball. But the maniacal desire to chase after any baseball that comes out of the park? Not so much.

Vangeloff shows a little after eleven. He figured (correctly) that the Cubs wouldn't be hitting much after the night game. He is wearing a Diamondbacks hat (51–111 in 2004). I ask him about "the Sosa Homer," which passes as a modern folktale out here. He walks me down Kenmore about seventy-five feet, where 536' is spray-painted on the asphalt. On June 24, 2003, Sosa hit a ball that landed, not rolled, on what everyone says is this exact spot. The next day, a local surveying crew used global positioning to measure the distance—the ball went 536 feet.

Vangeloff was the one who got it. He judged that the ball was going to land behind the crosswalk crowd, so he adjusted and ran behind them. The ball still sailed over him. But the initial lead he took was enough to secure him the ball. When it bounced into a flower bed, Vangeloff was there.

Ever since it was hit, people come to Waveland and Kenmore to ask where it landed. They usually end up asking Vangeloff, who will rarely, if ever, reveal that he has the ball at home. He figured Sosa or the Cubs might come asking for it. They never did.

When we get back to the crosswalk, a man with his family comes by. He wants to know "where Sosa's home run spot is." Vangeloff points the man, who looks rather eager, toward the spot we were standing in only seconds before. The man motions for his teenage daughters to follow. They look skeptical.

The family prompts a question. Does Vangeloff have one of his own waiting at home? He shakes his head no. Whenever he settles down, the woman will have to understand that this is who he is. He will not sacrifice his days or nights on Waveland.

"In 2003, a crew from *Nightline* came out, and they were doing a segment on the neighborhood because the Cubs were in the playoffs," says Vangeloff as Moe signals from inside that B.P. is about to start. "The reporter must have stood here and talked to me for about thirty or forty minutes. A few days later, it airs and I'm in it for about ten seconds.

"The reporter asks, 'How many balls have you caught,' and I say, 'About twenty-five hundred.' He immediately asks if I'm single, and I say yes. Those were my only two quotes. I'm like, '*great*'."

One of the inherent dangers in this whole game—and this is why I miss the first three street-landers today—is that a spot on Waveland puts you directly in the middle of a parade that includes the best-looking women in the Midwest. Vangeloff claims that his peripheral vision has improved because of this. He issues a warning, though: If two good-looking girls walk by, wait a few seconds before turning your head to follow them down the street.

"More often than not, those two girls will be on a double date and their boyfriends will be right behind them," he says. "You don't want them to see you doing it."

Only four balls fly out during batting practice. I am in contention for none of them. Vangeloff gets one by pinning it up against a school bus. The wind is blowing in from left field—the Ballhawks' worst scenario. By game time, Vangeloff has left. Mielke is at work, waiting for the extended Fourth of July holiday to begin. Only Moe, Buhrke, and Davison remain for the game. They don't expect many to be hit over the fence.

In the first inning, a man named Bill comes up and hands me a free ticket. Do I have a choice but to attend? I head in, only to find that my 500-level seat is directly behind a pole. On come the headphones, time to listen to Pat and Ron describe the parts of the park—namely, all of home plate—that I can't see.

It is a fantastic game. Kerry Wood makes his first start in almost two months, striking out nine and allowing just two hits in six innings of work. Todd Hollandsworth hits a game-winning single in the bottom of the ninth to give the Cubs a 3–2 win. The team is now 40–36 and two games behind Atlanta for the wild-card lead. With Wood and Prior appearing healthy, our hopes are again climbing.

June 30

The temperature is in the nineties for the second straight day. It's eleven a.m. and batting practice still hasn't started. Vangeloff and Buhrke are leaning up against the yellow building on Waveland. They have a theory for the delay.

"It looked like they were filming some movie in there," says Vangeloff, pointing inside the park. "Maybe it'll pick up later."

The movie in question is called *The Break Up* and stars Jennifer Aniston and Vince Vaughn. It has been shooting all over Chicago for the past few weeks. One of my acquaintances is in Wrigley right now, serving as an extra, earning a whopping $150 for a seventeen-hour day. He can only speak to Aniston if she speaks to him. Sadly, he later reports that Aniston stays silent.

Mielke is standing in his spot in front of the Budweiser building. He eyes the line for the bleachers. His report: "There's no good boobage out here today."

Batting practice starts and a few balls come out. Mielke gets two of the first three. I am so much worse than him, it is pitiful. Standing with these guys on Waveland is like stepping into the box against Maddux or Clemens. I don't stand a chance. On each of the last two opportunities, I only picked up the sight of the ball as Mielke was settling in underneath it.

A lot of people out here look like I did two days ago. They think they can grab a baseball for a souvenir. But after a while, you can see the realization come over their faces. They curse the Ballhawks under their breath. They start to pray for the ball to hit the ground. It's the only way they're snagging one.

The game starts and I still have no balls. (*Wait . . .*) But the wind is blowing out. The crowd thins. Most people head into the game, hopeful the Cubs' win streak will hit five games. I stay outside with Moe, Buhrke, Davison, and Mielke. George heads home because he has to work at his family's store, Dominguez Groceries, in Rogers Park. Vangeloff also has to work, so he's gone before the first pitch.

The Brewers and Cubs start out strong, each scoring five runs over the first four innings. A homer by Aramis Ramirez hits the left field fence but stays in the park.

I am standing in the middle of Waveland, playing catch with a man named Tom. He is wearing a Cincinnati hat and likes me to throw him pop-ups so he can field them. He throws low on a few occasions and the ball rolls all the way to the Sheffield intersection. Each time, a bouncer or patron from Murphy's picks it up and throws it back.

The Brewers take control of the game by the time Milwaukee broadcaster Bob Uecker sings the seventh-inning stretch. (His rendition is my favorite of the season: *"So it's root, root, root for the Brewers . . . You do the same for the Cubs!"*) By the eighth inning, everyone has left except for Davison. If a ball comes out here, it's between me, him, and a dozen motor coaches.

"A lot of baseballs come out here in the late innings," Davison says.

Davison takes Mielke's usual spot. I am in Vangeloff territory, near the crosswalk.

With the Brewers leading, Carlos Lee comes to the plate. Over my headphones, I hear a crack of the bat and a groan from Santo. The gradually turning heads in the bleachers reveal that the ball is going to fly out of the stadium.

There!

I pick up the ball. It's heading straight for Davison. He doesn't catch it on the fly. In pursuit, I head east down Waveland and . . . this is a real possibility . . . is my first ball really going to be a gamer?

I am, as the kids say, trucking. The ball hits up against the iron fence in front of the Budweiser house and bounces back onto the sidewalk. But just as I think I have a chance, Davison regains his footing and scoops it up.

In the bleachers, the sun-tired and drunken fans start hooting for Davison to throw it back. Fat chance. Davison returns to Waveland and Kenmore and, in one motion, scoops up a bogus ball from between the plugs of the fire hydrant. He takes three steps then launches it into Wrigley. It lands in the outfield and rolls toward the infield. The Bleacherites go crazy. Davison's motion is so fluid, so secretive, that no one spots the bait and switch.

"Idiots," Davison says.

I hang around for the rest of the game—a 10–6 Brewers win. I patrol the ground where Davison caught the ball from Lee. Like Vangeloff says, "This is like fishing with little kids. A ball lands somewhere and everyone goes over and puts their poles where the fish was caught."

It is sticky hot and I buy a bottle of water for the walk home. I am going home with nothing but my empty glove. After three days of work, I have no baseballs to show for it.

Stupid Ballhawks.

Yet for the first time, I think I can understand the allure of coming out here as a Ballhawk. Apart from buying a few Slurpees, I haven't spent any money over the past three days. I haven't had to mess with any scalpers. I haven't had to buy a ticket.

But I've been in the game. I guess you could even say I was at the game. I've made more neighborhood friends. We did some quality bullshitting. An essential truth became clear: Waiting for baseballs means you are always doing something.

Even if you are doing nothing.

Frequently Asked Questions

July

Q: *Do you miss your old job?*
A: I miss having a regular paycheck. I miss the big-time events—the state championships, helping out at the odd Royals game, gearing up for Chiefs season. But I don't miss trying to keep my head off the table at a Monday night girls' basketball game that ends with a score of 77–23. I don't miss covering silly stuff like auto racing, which is what I'd be covering this week if I were still in the Show-Me State. True story: One year I had to write a fan story about the NASCAR race that was in town. I approached a man who was wearing a Dale Jarrett hat and asked him for an interview. He hiccupped, then pushed his six-year-old son in front of my notepad. "I'm too drunk," he explained. "Talk to my boy." Oh, the "fan" stories. I don't miss those. And yes, I realize this whole book is a fan story. Then again, Cubs fans are my type of fans.

Q: *You said you missed your paychecks—are you low on cash? Do you need some?*
A: That has to be one from Dad. I'm still surviving on my book advance, which was $50 worth of food stamps, a Chicago Cubs painter's cap from the '80s, and a gift tin of popcorn.

Seriously, this town charges you to breathe. If it's not the scalpers, it's the bars. If it's not the landlord, it's the mayor, levying all sorts of car sticker fees for my ride.

Here's a surefire way to make $80 disappear: Start talking to a gaggle of flight attendants at Murphy's. Offer to buy drinks.

Q: *What's the best deal on food in the stadium?*
A: The frosty malt cup, without a doubt. But someone explain this to me, why does a bag of cotton candy cost $5? A malt cup is only $2.25. And there's a freezer involved with producing malt cups. Cotton candy is just sugar. Whatever the logic, the malt cup is the most delicious treat in the park. Even the wooden spoon they provide tastes good.

Q: *Don't the Cubs usually suffer from a June swoon? What happened?*
A: Well, they *were* only 13–13 in the month. But, as of June 30, the team's record stands at 40–37, two games behind wild-card leader Atlanta. With an eleven-game stretch against Washington, Atlanta, and Florida, this would be the time to make a move.

Chapter Eleven

Wild Bill Arrives from Arizona

July 1–3—vs. Washington

Here's the interesting thing about Wrigley Field: *Anybody* can become *somebody*. You don't need to be a power-hitting right fielder or a quotable shortstop or a brainy manager. No, anyone can carve out an identity for himself out here. The biggest example of this phenomenon is Harry Caray, a St. Louis orphan who is the only person honored by a statue on Wrigley's grounds. To put it in perspective, Cubs legends Ernie Banks, Billy Williams, and Ron Santo only have their numbers mounted on a flagpole.

Yet Caray is a bad example because he had the benefit of being broadcast on radio and television. Instead, look at the notoriety achieved by a guy like Ronnie Woo, who'd be just another bum if it weren't for the Cubs. Or "Bleacher" Bob, a middle-aged scalper who's the best-known pavement pounder out here. Or Moe Mullins, the Ballhawk who could double as a permanent street fixture if asked. All these guys, at some point, made a conscious decision that they would be defined through a baseball team. Know what? All of them seem content and happy and comfortable in their own skin.

And now it seems like another Cubs celebrity is about to be newly minted. "Wild Bill" Holden has been walking across the country since the beginning of January, and he's due to reach his destination—Wrigley Field—sometime before today's game.

Holden has already achieved quite a bit of fame, thanks to an article on ESPN.com last month. He's been in other papers, mostly when he's passed through towns on his way to Chicago.

Talk about questionable sanity. In early January, Holden, a fifty-six-year-old unemployed schoolteacher, stayed up late to watch a copy of *This Old Cub*, the documentary about his hero, Ron Santo, and his lifelong battle with diabetes. After watching the movie, which features some gripping scenes of Santo dealing with the loss of both of his legs, Holden decided that he needed to do something to raise money for the Juvenile Diabetes Research Foundation. So Holden, an out-of-shape man with two knees devoid of cartilage and in need of surgery, decided on the most logical thing: He would walk from Prescott Valley, Arizona, to the corner of Clark and Addison, a trip of more than twenty-one hundred miles.

The marathon trip is in Holden's nature. In the late '60s, he walked from Southern Illinois's campus in Carbondale to Chicago, a 330-mile trip, to raise money for the USO's tour through Vietnam. A few years later he rode a bike from Carbondale to Washington, D.C., to celebrate SIU's hundredth anniversary.

Then, the kicker: In 2000, he had tickets to the Cubs–White Sox series but no money for a plane or bus ticket. So he set out on his bike and rode to Wrigley Field.

Holden's goal for this trip is to raise $250,000 for JDRF. He's walked through Arizona, New Mexico, Texas, Oklahoma, Missouri, and now most of Illinois with only a cheap pair of Reeboks, a fanny pack, and several *This Old Cub* T-shirts. The *This Old Cub* staff back in Los Angeles lined up donations of hotels and meals. Holden's days averaged just a little over ten miles, six times a week.

This morning, his 172nd day on the road, Holden was seven miles away from Wrigley and the Cubs' Web site says he's walking down Lincoln Avenue for the rest of the way. It seems appropriate to welcome Wild Bill home.

It's just after ten a.m. and I'm walking north on Lincoln (a street west of Wrigley), hoping to catch Wild Bill and his group headed the other way. The weather is sunny but cool, a heaven-sent break for Holden after the scorchers of the past few days.

I'm not sure what to expect. Ten thousand people backing Holden on his final push? That's unlikely, but there's got to be a good group with him, right?

Wrong. When I finally spot Holden ambling through Lincoln Square, he's with four other people, and everyone's involved in producing a possible movie about Holden. Jeff Santo, who made *This Old Cub* about his father, is walking backward in front of Holden, clutching a small video camera.

Before I can get all the way to the group, Holden stops and settles into a patio chair along the sidewalk. The patio belongs to Costello Sandwich & Sides, about two and a half miles from Wrigley. A producer runs into the store to buy Holden a banana and some shelled peanuts.

I walk up and introduce myself to Wild Bill. Without pause, he welcomes me in a booming Irish tenor. His enthusiasm suggests that I'm the first person he's seen in twenty-one hundred miles. Of course this is far from the truth.

"Well hey, Kevin!" he says, gripping my hand. "I'm Bill Holden. It's real great to meet you!"

Holden has a head of white hair and a face as red as a Santa photograph. He's wearing the same thing I've seen in all the news clips: white *This Old Cub* shirt, mesh Cubs hat, fanny pack and shorts.

Looking over his left shoulder at Santo, Holden takes a deep breath.

"How much longer we got to go, Jeff?"

"Not much longer, Bill."

"All right."

With help, Holden rises to his feet and keeps walking south. He looks twenty years older than my father, but the true gap is only four. His halting step, combined with his doughy body, makes for a painful sight. It's beyond belief that he's walking from Costello's to Wrigley, let alone Arizona to Chicago.

I'm right beside him, yet hesitant to ask questions. Holden is having enough trouble breathing without talking. *Wheeze. Step. Wheeze. Step.*

Holden reaches the corner of Lincoln and Montrose. I am hanging back with Santo as he videotapes. A woman on a bike slams on her brakes.

"Hey, you're that guy that's walking . . . ," she says.

"Yes, ma'am," Bill says, and stops to chat.

"Bill, we're meeting the governor at twelve thirty," Santo reminds him.

"I gotta go," Holden says.

Illinois governor Rod Blagojevich will be waiting at the corner of Southport and Addison. Holden can make it on time, but there isn't time for dawdling.

Holden is originally from Elgin, a riverboat city along the Fox River, about ten minutes from my hometown. I ask him if he'd like to come back, if he misses Chicago.

"I'll go wherever they give me the opportunity to teach kids and maybe coach," Holden says. "But yeah, I'd like to come back."

A cement truck drives by and honks.

"All right, man! Way to go!"

There are some similarities between Holden's venture and my own. I'll admit that he is doing something for a good cause in the face of adversity, whereas I am punishing my healthy body by consuming vats of beer while harassing women at Wrigleyville bars.

But there was a certain blind faith involved in both of our steps and it started with the Cubs and Wrigley Field. For Holden, it goes a bit further. He used to teach at a Native American reservation and saw a few students affected by juvenile diabetes. After watching Santo's optimism during the filming of *This Old Cub*, he knew he could do something.

"But you're right," he says. "Wrigley Field is a magical place. You have no idea how long I've been thinking about just sitting down inside and drinking a few Old Styles."

The walk continues. I'm the only nonmovie person in the caravan. Holden tells everyone to wait when we reach the Wild Goose, a bar on Lincoln. He disappears into the bathroom. Five minutes pass, then six and seven. Our entourage starts getting a little nervous.

"Should someone go in there and check?" one of the producers asks.

Just then Holden walks through the door and two guys at the bar call out his name and offer him a drink.

"Not just yet, boys," says Holden, revealing a still-present Chicago accent. "Gotta go meet the governor."

Holden reaches the corner of Addison and Lincoln. It's a goose-bump moment for everyone present. Twelve more blocks and the journey is complete. Three cameramen join the group. Holden is ready for the occasion, having just put on a shirt that reads "JDRF—Find a Cure."

The words below that request another, if somewhat more trivial, goal.

"Ron Santo for H.O.F. Let Justice Prevail."

Holden's college buddy meets him at the corner. He's wearing a St. Louis Cardinals hat, but no matter. The two giant men grip each other in a bear hug.

"Want to go to Georgie Boy's for a beer?" says the man in the Cardinals hat, referring to Cubby Bear owner George Loukas, another SIU alum.

"Nah, we gotta go meet the governor," says Holden.

Five blocks later, Holden looks down a side street where Blagojevich, his daughter, and a host of aides are waiting.

"Governor! How are ya? I'm Bill Holden!"

Cubs fans are familiar with Blagojevich. In fact, the only time I ever see the governor is when he shows up at Wrigley Field. Would it be partisan to say he ran for the office simply because he wanted to attend more Cubs games?

For Blagojevich and his goofy haircut, it's a great photo opportunity. Holden seems genuinely impressed, so perhaps it isn't all that bad. But instead of cheers for Holden, people are now cheering for Blagojevich. What was once a solo man's journey across America has turned into an *event*, complete with security detail, paparazzi, and sprinting onlookers.

Clark and Addison.

Holden looks at the stadium marquee.

"Welcome Home 'Wild Bill' Holden," it reads.

Another goose-bump moment.

At the front gate is a gathering of Holden's family and friends. Everyone's cheering, and I'm no longer within six people of Holden. The entourage swarms toward the front gate and Holden steps inside.

Later, I will watch Holden on television as he enters the gate in right field and makes his way to throw out the first pitch, greeted by—who else?—Ron Santo. Seven innings later and Wild Bill's leading the crowd in the seventh-inning stretch. He looks like he's belonged in the booth all his life.

On the walk to Wrigley, Bill told me the day would be complete with a Cubs win. "I just know they're going to win it today," he said.

And yet not every dream comes true, because the Cubs seal a special day with a 4–3 loss to Washington. Welcome home, Wild Bill.

Meanwhile, the scalpers are finally doing what they're best at— making scads of money. The Fourth of July weekend is their time to shine. Everyone from the Midwest and beyond seems to be in the neighborhood. Throw in the Nationals' first appearance at Wrigley and you've got a sellers' market. I meet up with two college friends, Colin and Haydn. No scalper will sell three tickets together for less than fifty apiece and three innings later the prices still haven't dropped. As a backup plan, we hunker down on Murphy's patio and watch the action around the bleacher gate.

We inevitably tire of paying $16.50 for a round of three beers and head back to my porch to listen to Pat and Ron call the game on the radio. If the wind is blowing the right way, we can usually hear muffled cheers and the seventh-inning stretch. No such luck today.

The three of us set to work on two cases of beer, a purchase that cost less than two rounds at Murphy's. It is 2:45. Why are we drinking? Who knows, other than it is Friday, the holiday weekend is here, and we're the best-looking S.O.B.'s we know.

Four hours later, we are drunkenly arguing about why the Cubs haven't won in ninety-seven years, who slept with the ugliest girl in college, and whether new arrival Joe can hit the alley with a thrown beer bottle. (The answers being "because they suck," no clear consensus, and "Yes, now please put the bottle down.")

God bless summer.

We walk west toward Art and Angie's. The reason for our journey is simple. There is a Beanbag tournament going on.

Well, at least *I* call it Beanbag. You might know it as "Bags" or "Cornhole." Either way, it's a Chicago summer tradition on par with sixteen-inch softball and hanging out on Lake Michigan. On the way over here, we saw another sidewalk game going on. There are undoubtedly hundreds of others taking place across the city.

The rules are simple. Each participant throws a beanbag at an angled wooden board several feet away. The goal is to put the beanbag through a hole near the top of the board. If it makes it through, that's three points. If the bag comes to rest on top of the board, that's one. First to fifteen or twenty-one wins.

With tiki torches surrounding the yard and the sound of bags plopping on plywood, I conclude the game is popular for three reasons:

1. It is undoubtedly safer than the following backyard drinking activities: horseshoes, lawn darts ("the game the government took away," says Art), and "Let's Tease the Rottweiler."
2. It provides closure for those of us still upset about not being selected by Bozo for the Grand Prize Game.
3. One hand remains free, allowing everyone to hold a beer can while playing. (This being of obvious importance.)

Beanbag helps to distinguish us from the New Yorkers. In college, I knew two types of people: those who were moving to Chicago and those who were moving to Manhattan. The transplanted New Yorkers are now into playing grown-up. They attend overpriced clubs, pay outrageous amounts of rent with twelve of their closest friends, and start liking bands like Interpol and Arcade Fire.

Chicagoans throw beanbags at each other.

Exactly who holds the civic upper hand between the two cities is unclear.

A few hours later, when sobriety and reason have completely slipped away, we jump into a cab.

"Burrito House!" someone instructs.

With that, we are off.

Sunrise comes and I look down toward the white T-shirt on my chest. A bit of sour cream here. A fleck of burrito corn there. I'm still wearing jeans. My shoes are on my feet. There's a good possibility that four evil pixies have drilled two holes in the front of my brain and are now hammering away.

Advil doesn't do the trick. Neither does a big glass of water or a dry bagel. I download the damage from the digital camera to dissect exactly what happened. *Picture No. 26:* Haydn taking a leak in an alley a few blocks away. Fantastic. We are too old for this. But such a realization cures nothing.

Last night's action has sentenced me to an afternoon of watching the Cubs from the couch. Venturing outside might cause me to fall on the sidewalk, so I bemoan my fate and forge a promise.

I am never drinking again.

But it is a promise currently being repeated from bedroom and bathroom floors across the country, and it is an empty one. Made last weekend. And again the next.

In the past few weeks, I have tried to solicit explanations for the drinking festival that seems to be the norm for most twentysomething urban dwellers. It's understandable why past generations might have become alcoholics. Lack of diversions. The rise of the corner tavern. Blue-collar jobs that offered little reward except postwork beers.

On the opposite side is our generation, the one that lives in Wrigleyville, holds college degrees, works white-collar jobs and doesn't have the financial worries of someone who lived during the Depression.

A few weeks ago, during the Boston series, I walked home (drunk) with Omaha Ben, and we pondered the topic of overconsumption among the fairly privileged. At the time I was on day ten of a fourteen-day bender and could already feel my body begging me to stop, Roberto Duran style. In a bit of Jäger-inspired wisdom, Ben suggested our binges had to do with emboldening ourselves in otherwise awkward social situations.

"That's the problem with drinking . . . ," Charles Bukowski once wrote. *"If something bad happens, you drink in an attempt to forget; if something good happens, you drink in order to celebrate; and if nothing happens, you drink to make something happen."*

My generation falls into the last category. It gets ingrained when we are eighteen years old and living in Madison or Champaign or wherever and the people down the hall are getting ready for Thursday night with a big bottle of Captain Morgan that the guy with a fake ID managed to purchase.

The social reliance on alcohol continues once everybody discovers the bars and gains access to the right frat parties. Before you know it, you're twenty-six years old and pounding pregame Heinekens so you can tolerate standing in a crowded sausage-fest like the Mystic Celt on Southport Avenue. There must be a better way to pass the time, yet I (and this neighborhood in general) have failed to find it.

But should you listen to my whining, which is undoubtedly the product of a vicious hangover and having to watch a 4–2 Cubs loss from the confines of my puffy black sofa? As I never seem to have these reservations while cracking my fourteenth beer of the night, perhaps the answer is no.

To Wild Bill's presumable dismay, the Cubs lose Sunday's game 5–4 in twelve innings, negating perhaps the most exciting play of the season to date, a game-tying two-run homer by Aramis Ramirez in the bottom of the ninth with two outs.

And it gets worse, because the Cubs go to Atlanta and promptly lose four straight games, running the losing streak to eight games. It is obviously no way to establish dominance, and on July 7, the team's NL Central hopes are already on life support. A 40–44 record is bad enough to place the Cubs thirteen and a half games behind the St. Louis Cardinals, the reigning National League champs. The team is eight games out of the wild-card race.

The situation is certainly not what I had in mind when moving to Wrigleyville. But the Cubs finish the first half of the season with a three-game sweep in Florida, and hope receives some mouth-to-mouth. There are seventy-five games to go. Anything can happen.

(Actually, I'm getting tired of writing sentences like that.)

Chapter Twelve

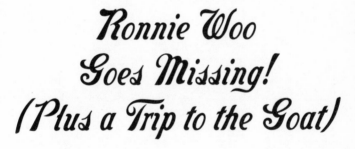

*Ronnie Woo
Goes Missing!
(Plus a Trip to the Goat)*

July 14–17—vs. Pittsburgh

I t's Thursday morning and the red message light on my cell phone is flashing. The screen reveals that someone called at 2:23 a.m. The "someone" happens to be Soks, my thirty-four-year-old buddy from the bleachers.

"Dude," is all he says before hanging up.

With the Pirates in town for a four-game set (today's game is a makeup), I arrange to meet Soks at the Full Shilling for a pregame beer and dog.

"Did you see I buzzed the tower last night?" he asks when I arrive.

"Soks, it's like this," I tell him, acknowledging his call. "You're too old to be calling me at two in the morning on a Thursday."

"Yeah, but you're too young to be sleeping through it," he says.

"Point taken."

I leave and head to Waveland and Kenmore, where George, the Ballhawk with the shark tattoo, sells me a bleacher for fifteen bucks. As we are talking, we are being filmed on a minicam by Mike Diedrich, who is shooting a documentary titled *Ballhawk*.

186 • KEVIN KADUK

Maybe it's a good thing the bleachers are being expanded. Some of these guys are becoming more famous than some of the players.

Seeing cameras and reporters outside the ballpark is all part of a normal day. Low on news and need a good filler feature? Head to Wrigleyville, where thousands of stories converge on a daily basis. I stopped asking camera crews what they were doing long ago. I still take interest in the Japanese crews, who come around more often than you think.

My conversation with George continues until we see a familiar figure—Wild Bill Holden—lumbering our way. He's dressed the same as he was thirteen days ago.

"Hey, Bill!"

"Kevin! How the heck are ya? I'm never going to forget you!"

We discuss the rest of Bill's big day, and he uses the following adjectives to describe it—"unbelievable," "unbelievable," and, oh yeah, "unbelievable."

"The whole thing was just unbelievable," he adds for good measure.

George Loukas has given Holden the use of an apartment in the yellow brick building on the corner of Waveland. Now Holden's life consists of walking around Wrigleyville and attending every game on the schedule. Holden doesn't know when or if he's headed back to Arizona. He doesn't have a lot of money to his name. When I ask for his cell phone number, he says it'll be useless in a week because he hasn't been able to pay the bill.

"Well, how can I take you out for breakfast?" I ask him.

"See that window over there?" Holden asks, pointing to his current digs on the first floor. "Just come over and knock on it. I'll most likely be there."

Deal.

"I'm serious, Kevin," he says. "I'll never forget you."

Over the next two weeks, I will knock on the window three

different times, but Holden never answers and I wonder how his season ended up.

The Cubs are back from the All-Star break and hopefully poised for a second-half run. But the return of the team is far from the biggest Wrigleyville news. On June 29, a woman claiming to be Ronnie Woo's wife reported to Chicago police that the Cubs superfan was missing. When that report came to light on Wednesday, everyone started speculating about his whereabouts.

But the story, despite huge placement in the *Tribune* and its youth-oriented tabloid *RedEye*, didn't have legs. After reading the report online, I clicked on a message board, where a poster reported seeing Ronnie at a White Sox game. By mid-afternoon, the whole story was debunked, and Ronnie emerged to say that he didn't even have a wife.

"I was just on All-Star break," Ronnie said. "Just like most players."

The news of Ronnie being "found" was big news again this morning, and in the middle of the game he appears in the bleachers to cheers and high fives.

"Good to see you, Ronnie!"

"Hey, Ronnie, where'd you go?"

"Ronnie, did you see the newspapers? You're a star!"

Ronnie keeps walking, slapping hands on his way to left field. "I'm alive! *Woo!* I'm alive! *Woo!*"

A few feet away, Mark, the Ballhawk who reminds me of Anthony Kiedis, shakes his head.

"That dude's crazy," he says. "Sometimes he'll look at me and it'll seem like he remembers me. Other times, it's just a blank look. I guess it doesn't matter either way. I try to help him out. Everyone around here does. We sent him to Yankee Stadium for the Cubs series."

Mark is standing in his usual spot, last row in the left field bleachers, right around where the large fence ends. He's wearing a glove, but not a shirt. He's got a couple of girlfriends with him.

Standing outside on Waveland doesn't work for Mark, even though he got Sosa's 514th home run, the one that left him with a concussion. He'd rather be inside the stadium, watching as the game unfolds. Being in the stands also gives him the opportunity to catch the balls thrown by players after the mid-inning warm-ups. Later, when Todd Hollandsworth enters the game, he throws the ball straight to Mark, who responds with a leaping grab. It helps to become friendly with the players.

Mark is twenty-five years old and a day manager at a Home Depot. He heads to Wrigley for night games and whatever day games he can make. A former college ballplayer, Mark still harbors some diamond dreams. He tells me he has a minor league tryout scheduled for the fall.

"As far as I'm concerned, baseball's the greatest game out there," Mark says, his eyes never coming off home plate. "And the Cubs are the best franchise in the majors. I grew up in Chicago, then moved to Wisconsin. I had to move back because the commute to Wrigley was too much of a haul.

"I love playing baseball and I don't plan on stopping. I've got a tryout, so who knows what can happen?"

Thirty yards away, twenty-three-year-old Matt Murton is making his Wrigley Field debut for the Cubs. His red hair is tucked underneath the blue Cubs cap, and he's blown a wad of pink gum into a sloppy bubble.

For the first time all season, I find myself wishing for a postgame Q&A session with a player. What was going on in Murton's head for his first home start? Did he have the same kind of giddy enthusiasm that Mark would have if given the chance to leave the bleachers and play an inning on the field?

These are the types of questions that often run through my

mind. Just how committed are Cubs players to the cause? Do they really understand the hope and longing instilled after ninety-seven years of championship-less baseball? Or would a title with, say, the Mariners count just as much as one with the Cubs for them?

The answer, I assume, is probably both. Ron Santo hails from Washington, but he's become a bigger fan than those who listen to his broadcasts. On the other hand, how could Randall Simon, a late-season acquisition in 2003, come to understand North Side suffering in such a short stint?

The Cubs go on to beat the Pirates 5–1 behind eight innings of two-hit ball from Mark Prior. Ten "K" placards hang on one of the Waveland rooftops, signifying Prior's ten strikeouts. At 44–44, the Cubs are back at .500.

With more than half the season already in the books, I think it's safe to say that Wednesday and Thursday afternoons are my favorite days to attend games. The weekends are fun, but attract too many tourists and casual fans who just want to party. It's always easy to get tickets on Monday and Tuesday, but night games are a secondary attraction.

For me, Wrigley Field is best at 3:15 in the middle of the week and Cubs runners on second and third. That's when you start to think about the people around you, nearly forty thousand people on their way to a good time. And then you think about the people who *are* at work and listening to the game on the radio or watching icons on an Internet GameCast. Wednesday and Thursday games are weekends built into the middle of the week. They're for making you feel like you're getting away with something.

Jen Chen, a friend from Kansas City, comes to town on Friday, and she's just in time. For the most part, everyone I've talked with this season has been to Wrigley many times before. Jen is a Wrigley Field virgin.

She loves the NFL, but her love for baseball has been dampened by the continued suckitron that is the Kansas City Royals. When we get to the game, her first observation is a doozy.

"I think Pirates fans should wear eye patches," Jen says.

"Good idea," I respond. "And if that works out, they can all get parrots to perch on their shoulders."

"Ooooh!" Jen's face lights up.

We are sitting in the upper deck in $38 seats (stupid July pricing) that afford a good lay of the land. I try to focus Jen on the question at hand: First impressions of Wrigley Field?

"I love it," she says. "It's just so old-school. There's no Jumbotron. No 'Kiss Cam.' The Budweiser sign on that house is great. It's much smaller than I thought it might be, and look at how many people are out here on a Friday afternoon! Doesn't anyone work around here? This would never happen in Kansas City."

"So is Wrigley better or worse than you expected?" I ask.

"It's much better," says Jen, sipping on a Bud Light. "You come here and you have a mental picture in your head, but you don't realize how everything's immersed in the Wrigley atmosphere. It sounds kind of clichéd, but you kind of get chills."

The game is a laugher. The Cubs score three runs in both the second and third innings, then put things away with a five-run sixth inning that completes an 11–1 victory over the Pirates. This type of game is anticlimactic, but preferable to the close ones the Cubs have lost over the past month. Today feels like a hot shoe at a blackjack table. Everything's going right, people are high-fiving and drinking, and you can't possibly imagine a time when you'll actually lose a hand. This is the feeling we're left with after the victory. It lasts until Saturday, when the Pirates pull a string of five-card 21s, winning 3–0 on a hot and hazy afternoon that we spend at North Avenue Beach, listening to the game on the radio.

* * *

On Sunday, Jen and I hop on the southbound Red Line and head downtown. We navigate the shopping crowds on Michigan Avenue before descending into a dark cement staircase near a sign that reads, "World Famous Billy Goat Tavern & Grill—Butt in Any Time."

The place belongs to Sam Sianis, a squat Greek with a hooked nose and the thickest accent you've heard from someone who's been stateside since the '60s. Sianis inherited the place from his uncle, "Billy Goat" Sianis, the original proprietor. The Billy Goat isn't in Wrigleyville,* but it's definitely part of "Cubdom," or whatever you want to call it.

By now, most every sports fan knows the story. In 1945, Billy Goat Sianis tried to enter game one of the World Series with his pet goat, a creature he towed around town to promote his tavern on the West Side, near Chicago Stadium. Sianis and his goat were famously rejected from the park, so he sent a telegram to P. K. Wrigley that he was putting a curse on the team. The Cubs haven't been to the World Series since.

"World Famous" gets thrown around rather easily, but in the case of the Billy Goat, the claim might actually be true. We enter the venerable tavern, once a favored hangout of Chicago's newspapermen (the Tribune Tower and old Sun-Times building is/was located nearby), only to find a group of Japanese tourists snapping furiously away on their black Nikons. The Cubs are in the middle of a five-run third-inning rally, and a few people at the bar are clapping. We step up to the suspiciously silent grill (it is Sunday, after all) and order two *cheezborgers*, which will later be

---

*People often assume—and I've been asked for walking directions from Wrigley—that the Billy Goat and Harry Caray's are near the park. Not even close. "You've got to take the Red Line into the city," I tell them. "Are you sure?" they always ask. Yes, I'm sure. There used to be a Billy Goat on Clark near Wrigley, but it wasn't the Billy Goat.

204 • KEVIN KADUK

sheathed in wax paper. When they come hot off the grill, we drown the burgers in ketchup and pile on the pickles and onions. We take a seat in the orange and green seats near the wall on the opposite side of the bar.

Everyone's got a few favorite places in the world, and this is one of mine. I'll admit that it's a haven for tourists. Appearances at the Taste of Chicago, the famous *Saturday Night Live* sketch, and frequent mentions in Mike Royko's columns have forever taken care of any foot-traffic problems. But when places get big, the impulse is to pour some of the profits back into the business and make the place look presentable for *future* tourists. Streamline the business, you know. Give it a nice spit and polish.

That will never happen at the Billy Goat. Because once the darkness snatches you from the bleak sunlight above, you find yourself in a place where twenty-first-century progress or materialism fails to impress the Greek immigrants behind the grill. Down here, a Coach bag is just a sack belonging to Mike Ditka. And Louis Vuitton? He's the new defenseman for the Blackhawks, right?

The authenticity at the Goat is real, not manufactured. Where else would you find a broken-down ATM (the kind that charges $2.50 service fees) covered with a black garbage bag? At the bar, you can buy mini-pints of Jack or J&B to place in your pocket for the blustery trip back down Michigan Avenue. Thin strips of yellowed paper with boldfaced names of famous Chicago newsmen—Ward, Condon, Telander, Kass—provide decoration on a mirror. Over it all is a stuffed goat's head, which looks so ratty you don't want to glance at it while tearing through that chewy hamburger bun.

Mike Royko is a big reason I'm here—both as a patron and a journalist. He used to hold court by the bar, perhaps on the very stool where I sit and try to imagine the famous columnist mixing with cronies, political hacks, and pressmen with fresh ink on their pants. I'm not alone in this regard. Try to find a Chicago-born writer who doesn't list Royko among the top one or two influences.

Arguably the most consistent city columnist ever, Royko weaved together stories of Mayor Daley's political machine, the follies of big corporations, and the city's immigrant experience. As any regular reader would know, Royko was as big a Cubs fan as they come, and a good portion of his eight thousand columns dealt with the team's shortcomings on the North Side.

Royko died in the spring of 1997, and his last column was a look at why the Cubs hadn't won a World Series in his lifetime. The title drought had nothing to do with the Billy Goat curse, he claimed, but rather with the Cubs' reluctance to sign black players after Jackie Robinson broke baseball's color barrier in 1947. It wasn't until six years later, when the Negro Leagues had been stripped of good talent, that the Cubs finally got around to signing two black players.

Royko was tight with both Billy Goat and Sam Sianis, but objective enough to see the curse for what it was—a genius marketing masterstroke from two Greek immigrants who were much smarter than they let on. Take a look at the walls of the Billy Goat, where separate pictures of Sam with Bill and Hillary Clinton hang alongside giant blown-up Royko columns that focus on the Billy Goat. Does this strike you as a place that shrinks away from publicity?

And yet the Billy Goat curse continues to pick up steam. There is any number of people selling goat-related souvenirs outside Wrigley every day, and the casual fan seems to think it's "cute." The whole thing gained steam in 2003, when the media focused solely on the curses of the Cubs and Red Sox. Upon arriving at Wrigley for game six, I found Sam and Ronnie Woo performing some sort of exorcism on a goat outside the ballpark, for the benefit of the cameras and reporters swarming around them. But if you're a Chicagoan, you know any number of goat exorcisms have been performed over the years. None of them has worked.

To lend credence to the Billy Goat curse is to ignore a few key facts:

- By the time the curse was set upon the Cubs in 1945, the team had already gone thirty-seven years without a World Series title.
- Cubs owner P. K. Wrigley was an inept baseball man who focused on pushing the image of "beautiful Wrigley Field" instead of building a good product on the field.
- Three words: Brock for Broglio.

Is there a curse? Genuine Cubs fans don't want to believe so, because if there were, there'd be no reason to watch. And besides, we like to think we're a little smarter than to believe in intellectual hocus-pocus. Hard work will overcome anything. The Cubs organization just has to want to work hard enough to get it. Whether they do all they can is up for debate.

Until then we'll sit at Billy Goat, order another double, cheeps, not fries, and another Coke, no Pepsi. The Cubs win 8–2 and Jen drags me to Michigan Avenue, where I sit at H&M for an hour and a half while she picks out one $12 shirt. Jen is a big sports fan, but a girl's real interests can only be held at bay for so long.

July 25–27—vs. San Francisco

It's been a slow month in Wrigleyville. The Cubs have only played seven home games thus far; the rest of the time has been taken up by the All-Star break and trips to Atlanta, Florida, Cincinnati, and St. Louis.

The neighborhood without the Cubs is a hard place to explain. After a while, you stop noticing the stadium when you pass by it. Well, that's not totally true. Passing an empty Wrigley always registers in your brain.

Hey, you think, *there's Wrigley Field.*

What fails to compute is that it's *freakin' Wrigley Field.* The center of the baseball universe. A field of dreams for people across the world. When you live in the neighborhood, it's just another feature. Maybe the best feature a neighborhood could have, but still an everyday sight nonetheless.

When it's empty, I try to imagine the grandstands packed and the buzz of the crowd. This can be a hard thing to do, especially when you're staggering home from the Red Line after a rough night of acting like a jerk in Lincoln Park. It can still be done. My secret is to imagine the crack of the bat and a ball hitting the pack of Ballhawks on Waveland. How that will work in February, when we're covered in snow, remains to be seen.

Wrigley Field always draws people, regardless of whether the Cubs are in town. Rare is the time when no one's taking a picture by the Harry Caray statue or in front of the red marquee.* This always makes me sad, because a picture is a poor substitute for attending a game, and it doesn't seem fair when someone's vacation doesn't match up with the Cubs' home schedule.

One day, I approached a couple who were passing a camera between themselves and taking pictures of each other on the far corner of Clark and Addison. I offered to take a picture so they could be in the shot together.

"That'd be great," said Bob, who was with his wife, Kathy. They were from outside Orlando and this was their first visit to Chicago.

---

*By the way, the red marquee officially reads "Wrigley Field: Home of Chicago Cubs." Notice the absence of "the" between "of" and "Chicago." For some reason, I like this, as it reflects the minimalism of a past generation.

"Disappointed that the Cubs aren't in town?" I asked.

"Definitely," Kathy said. "But we figured we'd come up here and see [Wrigley] for ourselves anyways. We were just saying that next time we come, we're going to make sure to check the schedule first."

"Are you guys Cubs fans?"

"Isn't everyone?"

There were still things for Bob and Kathy to see. The towering plywood souvenir stand was open at the corner of Clark and Waveland. All the bars and restaurants were open, with the Cubs against the Yankees playing on the plasma screens inside.

On most weekends, the Cubs run tours of Wrigley Field at $20 a head, but it's not a suitable replacement for a real, live game. My first visit to Camden Yards was on a ballpark tour, and while it was enjoyable to see where Cal Ripken once hung his jock, I would have preferred a doubleheader against the Yankees or Red Sox.

After a 4–3 road trip to Cincinnati and St. Louis, the Cubs return home. Once again, their inconsistency is startling. The team took the first two games against the Reds before dropping the last two, both easily winnable. Then, after wasting a good effort from Carlos Zambrano, the Cubs won Saturday's and Sunday's games against the Cardinals, capping the series with an extra-innings grand slam by Neifi Perez that won the game.

But despite the good feelings, everyone around Wrigleyville has become frustrated with the Cubs' inability to put together a winning streak of any kind. Splitting a series against the Reds? Then dominating the defending NL champions at Busch Stadium? If the Cubs were a group of doctors, they'd be nailing heart transplants while bungling cases of the chicken pox.

The series with San Francisco has been highly anticipated, but not for the reasons we thought in the preseason. To the disappointment of the Ballhawks (particularly Andy Mielke), Barry

Bonds has been on the disabled list the entire season and won't be making the trip, much less taking batting practice.

But as Cubs fans, we are drumming our fingertips together in evil Mr. Burns–like fashion. LaTroy Hawkins is making his first visit to Wrigley since being traded almost two months ago. Hawkins blew nine saves in thirty-four chances in 2004, and three before being traded this season. Now that he's no longer wearing blue pinstripes, you can tell that people are really ready to tee off on him. He thought the booing was bad as a Cub? Just wait.

On the way to Monday's night game, there's a different feeling in the air. It's a sense of urgency, one that's been absent from the crowd since the beginning of the season, when it seemed like our enthusiasm could will our way to a division title before the end of April. Right now the Cubs are 50–48, bad enough to be twelve games behind St. Louis but good enough to be four and a half behind the wild-card lead.

Cubs rookie Rich Hill makes his first major league start, and from section 223 I watch as he throws five innings of two-run ball. The Giants lead 2–1 going into the bottom of the eighth. At the beginning of the inning, we hear a rumble coming from the right field bullpen area. It's Hawkins, and he's entering the game in relief.

The response is beyond my imagination. The crowd's reaction— and I'm happily booing along with them—is like Kenneth Lay returning to Enron headquarters. The booing is admittedly cathartic, and you can tell everyone's having a grand old time participating. I'd like to report that little old ladies were spitting and cursing, but truthfully I didn't see any. Somewhere, though.

Hawkins immediately gives up a single to Todd Walker. A cheer goes up. The relieving exile looks unfazed, and he gets Derrek Lee to ground into a fielder's choice. San Francisco manager Felipe Alou pulls Hawkins for Scott Eyre, and Hawkins's trudge to the dugout is met with another round of derision. Four batters (and three pitchers) later, Neifi Perez singles Jeromy Burnitz home with the tying run. LaTroy Hawkins is charged with the run. In the ninth inning, Burnitz comes to the plate with the bases loaded and one out. Burnitz lifts a high fly ball to mid center field. Jason Ellison catches it and prepares for the throw home.

Everyone's holding their breath, turning toward center field, toward third, and then home. Ronny Cedeno comes charging down the line toward home and the ball arrives at roughly the same time. Cedeno slides and . . . safe! Wrigley Field is up for grabs, and I find myself high-fiving the guys behind me, our first (and last) interaction of the night.

It's a classic Chicago finish, and with the echoing crowd and the surrounding darkness, I use the excitement to summon a view of what Harry Caray would be doing right now. In my memory, he's reckless and hoarse-voiced, overcome by emotion, not sure of what to say, like the rest of us in the stands. *"Cubs win! Cubs win! Cubs win!"*

Tuesday's game rolls around and I have yet to leave my couch. Outside it's raining steadily, a nice respite from the scorching drought of a Midwest summer. On the television, Len Kasper and Bob Brenly are again sitting in the press box while the giant blue tarp rests on the field in the background. The broadcasting duo is trying to pass time by interviewing a sportswriter, and it's apparent they're waiting for a reel of baseball bloopers or an episode of *This Week in Baseball* to save them. The cameras pan around the stands, and most of the drenched masses are families who have nowhere else to go. Meanwhile, most of the childless fans are in the Cubby Bear or Murphy's, waiting for the pulling of the tarp.

This is where living a few blocks from Wrigley comes in handy. Instead of being trapped in a wet baseball stadium, I am completely dry and watching a *Real World: Austin* marathon. When the rain doesn't relent, I assume the game is canceled. This is good news: There will be a doubleheader tomorrow and I have nice seats in the 100 level behind home plate.

But 9:30 comes around, and through my channel-flipping I see the tarp is coming off. The game is actually going to be played. My roommate Dan and I throw on long-sleeve shirts and book to the stadium.

We start looking for tickets, and the quicker, the better. Greg Maddux is starting, and with two strikeouts he will become only the ninth pitcher with three hundred wins and three thousand Ks. The first pitch comes at 9:48, the latest start in Wrigley Field history. We make one lap around the field and find no tickets. There's a roar and the scoreboard on the right field says Maddux recorded his first strikeout. He needs only one more. We quicken our pace.

No tickets on lap two, or lap three. Everyone with tickets is either inside the park or gone home for the night. The Sheffield scalpers are nowhere to be seen. The top of the third inning comes, and as we walk east on Waveland, it happens. A roar of the crowd and a 2 turning into a 3 under the strikes category on the scoreboard. Omar Vizquel gets caught looking and Maddux's name is etched deeper in the record books. Dan and I are left on the outside. So much for being witnesses to history.

Inside, the crowd maintains a standing ovation for Maddux, the prodigal pitcher who returned to the Cubs after eleven seasons and three Cy Young Awards with the Atlanta Braves. "Mad Dog" pitched for the Cubs between 1986 and 1992, and the belief around Wrigley is that he is a member of the Cubs pantheon, like Ernie Banks or Ryne Sandberg, no matter what he achieved in Atlanta (namely a World Series title in 1995).

Maddux is "our kind of guy." Or at least my type of guy. He's six feet tall and weighs 180 pounds. He used to wear glasses on the mound, and if you saw him on the street you'd figure him for a C.B.O.T. trader or maybe a mid-level analyst at Ernst & Young.

But when he takes the mound, Maddux is a surgeon, relying on an exceptional changeup and pinpoint control of nearly every other pitch he throws. A scout once said that Maddux is so good that "we should all be wearing tuxedos when he pitches."

Or as Steve "Psycho" Lyons once famously said about Maddux's notorious fast pace (and I paraphrase): "If you're taking a date to a baseball game, it's best if Greg Maddux is pitching. If the date is going badly, the game will be over in two hours. And if the date is going well? *The game will be over in two hours.*"

We find tickets, five bucks apiece, in the bottom of the third inning. The park is surprisingly crowded for the late time, but there are plenty of good seats to be had. Two hundred level behind home plate is the best we can do. There cannot be a baseball stadium where the good seats are as relentlessly guarded as those at Wrigley. On the whole, Wrigley's seat ushers are an eagle-eyed crew. With an average age of eighty-four and zero tolerance for bullshit, these ushers are the type who'd turn away an eight-year-old from an empty section in the eighth inning. Or the type who'd ask for a ticket when a fan's hands are full of beers and nachos and they've already shown their tickets at least three or four times. (And yes, I'm still bitter from an incident in 1990, when a Wrigley Field usher wouldn't let me down by the dugout to get Tim Raines's autograph during All-Star Monday.)

The game is tied at one through six innings and the atmosphere at Wrigley is one of the most enjoyable of the year. All the sunshine bunnies have been chased home and last call for beer was at 9:20 (a half hour before game time), so the drunks have also been scared off. This leaves an enthusiastic bunch that is there only for baseball, and as the analog clock on top of the scoreboard creeps to midnight, everyone is hoping for a Cubs win. A couple next to us says they deserve to see a victory because they've waited so long. Who can argue with them?

An RBI single by J. T. Snow gives San Francisco a 2–1 lead in the top of the seventh inning. But Hawkins enters the game in the eighth—to another round of thundering boos—and promptly gives up a first-pitch, game-tying homer to catcher Michael Barrett. Ah, Hawkins blowing another save. It feels like old times.

But the game goes to extra innings, and the Cubs again display their complete lack of killer instinct. Jason Ellison hits an RBI single in the top of the eleventh, giving the Giants a 3–2 victory and shutting out Maddux and his fans on an otherwise special night. The clock now reads 1:15 a.m. We decide to get a postgame drink—"Just one," we say—but when we reach the stoop of Casey Moran's, we are met by a bouncer's outstretched palm.

"We're done for the night, guys," he says. "Closed."

Which brings up an interesting question: If the Cubs play a game and there was nowhere to drink after the game, did it ever really happen?

Frequently Asked Questions

August

Q: *By my count, there were five more games left in July—one with San Francisco and four against Arizona. What happened?*

A: I attended that Wednesday game against San Francisco—a 4–3 Cubs win, by the way—with a "lady friend" and one of her gal pals. We hit Casey Moran's afterward, where a college friend was drinking with coworkers from his summer law firm. Score one against America's litigators as we snuck several Miller Lites and rum and Cokes on the monstrous tab of a downtown firm. Several hours later, I was smooching with the aforementioned lady friend. Never underestimate the power of the Cubs when wishing to lay the smack with a milk-fed Midwestern girl. Just ask the guy in Sluggers who slow dances to Led Zeppelin's "Fool in the Rain" with a sweaty, feather-banged honey from Schaumburg. Now *that's* romantic.

As for being absent for the entire Arizona series, you'll understand once the next chapter begins. I didn't miss much, though. The Diamondbacks took three of four.

Q: *You've been suspiciously quiet about your dealings with the ladies. Why?*

A: While I'd love to delight you with some Henry Milleresque tales, the ladies' well has been surprisingly dry as of late. (I say surprisingly because I fancy myself a young Rick Sutcliffe, only sexier and without the big red beard, Cy Young Award or ESPN announcing gig.)

Truth is that meeting the ladies down here is a little harder than I expected. Either the women are out looking for bankers and real estate dudes and not guys who are "writing a book about Wrigleyville and looking to do some firsthand research about making out with a lady in the Cubby Bear bathroom," or else they are so stupidly drunk that trying to hook up with them would constitute a crime even in Thailand.

That said, I've been on a few dates. Among the highlights:

- Cutting myself with a razor an hour before a date and arriving at Penny's Noodle Shop with a mess of blood still running from my chin. Date at the Cubs game goes so-so, but I vow not to call the girl until my face wound heals. Later forget to call the girl, but she was a bit of a dope anyway. (And yes, I just called a girl a "dope.")

- Heading to Ivy on Clark for a "few drinks" with an old friend. It's karaoke night and I sing "California Girls," even though I shouldn't. Bartender gives us a free round of shots, which primes the lady friend's pump. She orders about six more, including several for the patrons around us. End up dragging said girl back to her apartment near Belmont, but not before she orders $17 worth of food at Clark Street Dogs and attempts to make out with the fry cook. (Details admittedly hazy on this one.)

- Meeting a possible dream girl at the Old St. Pat's Block Party, but forgetting to get her number, so I wait outside the gates, all stalker like and full of hope that she would finally pass by. When she finally does, she asks if I'm from Wisconsin. I tell her no and she eagerly gives up the digits. I wait the mandatory three days to call her but never get a return phone call. Grieve for the next three weeks. (Okay, not really.)

Q: *In the past few months you've used these FAQs to air a few grievances. Which complaint will you lodge this month?*
A: I actually have two.

1. You can go back through this entire book and not find a reference to Chicago's team as "the Cubbies." (It makes me shiver to even see that word on my screen.) First off, calling a group of grown men by that name has to be fairly emasculating, and maybe it's the sole reason for the team's poor mark the last century or so. Second, all the bandwagon fans seem to refer to the team in this fashion. As in "I love the Cubbies! Now, would you wear these billowy pants or this cute jean skirt with my striped retro Cubbies T-shirt?" If you're going to go with an alternate effeminate name for the Cubs, I prefer "The Small Bears."

2. Old Style beer. While this book is partly responsible for helping romanticize the product of G. Heilemen Brewing Company, I actually believe it tastes like a loaf of bread in a glass. And that's the best comparison I can think of. At some point, someone decided that Old Style and Cubs baseball went hand in hand. Then idiot kids like myself overlooked the fact that it tasted terrible

and instead thought it was "funny" and "ironic" that we were drinking the same beer as our fathers and grandfathers. This was great for Heileman Brewing of La Crosse, Wisconsin, which would otherwise find itself lumped with the Schlitzes, Falstaffs, and Hamms of the brewing world.

Q: *OK, what about a few raves to balance things out a bit?*
A: Again, all the raves are about Derrek Lee. Although he's fallen a bit off the Triple Crown pace (Andruw Jones has taken a commanding lead in the home run category), Lee is in the middle of becoming a superstar. There's nothing like watching a baseball player suddenly "get it" at the plate. Combine that with a humble personality, a hard work ethic in the batting cage, and no suspicion of steroid use, and you've got a hero that you can point out to aspiring players.

I've also got to hand a shout-out to the man who sells peanuts with a megaphone outside the main entrance. "Fuuh-rrrresh, deee-licious peeeee-nuts," he sings over and over again. He might be the happiest person on the planet, and for that he always gets my three dollars. If I've learned anything from the street vendors, it's that you've got to hustle to make a buck out here in Wrigleyville.

Chapter Thirteen

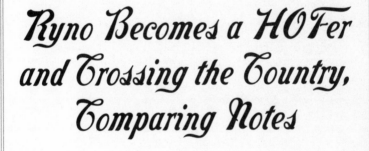

*Ryno Becomes a HOFer
and Crossing the Country,
Comparing Notes*

July 31–August 5

New York City, Cooperstown, Baltimore, Philadelphia, Pittsburgh, Cleveland, and Detroit

Spend enough time in Wrigley Field and you'll start to believe that it's the only stadium that matters. Those other locales, the parks that churn out highlights for *Sports Center*? They don't really exist, at least not in the "treasured classic" sense. It took a while for me to realize it, but it's more than just Chicagoans who value Wrigley Field.

Ever since Camden Yards threw open its gates in Baltimore, the retro ballpark has run rampant through the major leagues. Fourteen new stadiums have opened since 1992, and every single one has tried to re-create the "old-time" baseball experience with asymmetrical field dimensions, seats that hug the field, and larger-than-life scoreboards.

And yet something remains missing for the patrons of these multi-hundred-million-dollar stadiums. You can't throw baseball back to the '40s with high-definition ad boards on the facades and two decks full of wide luxury boxes above you.

So, looking to re-create the retro experience as closely as possible, baseball fans keep flocking to Wrigley and Boston's Fenway Park. It's impossible to estimate how many out-of-towners are at each Cubs game, but I offer up the following anecdote. Earlier in

the summer, while sitting in the bleachers, I noticed that everyone I was talking with was from another state. Michigan. Nebraska. New York. Connecticut. At one point, I stood up and
asked if everyone from Chicago or its suburbs would please raise
their hands. A grand total of two hands shot into the air. An in-
formal survey of twenty-five people revealed that everyone was
from somewhere other than the surrounding area.

The out-of-town visitors haven't been completely spared from
modern-day improvements, because Wrigley has had a few addi-
tions over the years, starting with the simple skyboxes that hang
from the grandstand and continuing to this season's rotating ad
board behind home plate.

And as mentioned before, Wrigley will change even more next
season, with the addition of more seats in the bleachers, and a
parking garage/museum along Clark Street that will open in the
future.

At any rate, since I have remained largely untouched by the
wave of retro stadiums, I decided it was time to hit the road and
compare stadium notes.

Were the conveniences of large concourses, expansive bathrooms, and built-in restaurants worth the sacrifice of Wrigley's
ambience, charm, and history? Could the manufactured atmo-
spheres surrounding the parks in Philly and Pittsburgh match up
with the authentic mood on Chicago's North Side? Would
Wrigley seem old and crumbly by comparison?

The trip seemed a natural, and I had a great jumping-off point,
the induction of Ryne Sandberg into the Hall of Fame in Cooperstown, New York. From there, the dominoes aligned just right. The
Yankees were playing at home the day before the induction. After
that we could hit Baltimore to see the Orioles play the White Sox,
and then head to Philadelphia, where the Cubs would play a day
later. Then, rapid-fire, Pittsburgh, Cleveland, and Detroit.

Seven days, six ballparks, a whirlwind research tour.

And so, on July 29, friend-for-life Polish Joe and I packed up my 2001 Ford Mustang with a cooler of soda, a Costco-sized junk food load, and a week's supply of clean underwear. We also had a GPS system that sometimes worked, the *Tribune*'s guide to Cooperstown, and a $5 coupon for Subway that Polish Joe's mom gave us. For trips like these, it was best to be prepared.

July 30

After nearly eight hundred miles on I-80, we arrive in Manhattan, where we'll park our car, take the subway to Yankee Stadium for an afternoon date with the Angels, and then return for dinner in the Village with an old friend.

We hop on the D Train, and the Yankees' fans' T-shirts reflect the attitude of an arrogant older brother who just dropped a driveway pickup game to a younger sibling. New Yorkers aren't taking Boston's World Series title particularly well.

"One title in 86 years is nothing to be proud of," reads one. "Yankees 26, Red Sox 5," says another, in reference to their respective title counts. "There never was a curse . . . the Red Sox just sucked for 86 years," ranks as my favorite. If the Cubs ever win a World Series, there will be a lot of money made selling these T-shirts in St. Louis.

A sellout crowd of over fifty-five thousand is expected in the Bronx, which is stickier, dirtier, and smellier than imagined in my Midwestern mind. The lady at the ticket window says only obstructed view seats are available, and for $75 we can sit on folding chairs located behind a large wall.

We turn our attention toward the scalpers, and I'm not

intimidated. I assume the secondary market is a lot like Wrigley's, and I am the best buyer in the world. Yet when a half hour passes and no reasonably priced tickets present themselves, a figurative trickle of urine starts to run down my leg. I turn into the tourist looking for any way in, and when a scalper offers bleachers for $35, three times face, there's nothing to do but accept the offer. That some athletes wilt under the pressure of a Big Apple spotlight suddenly makes a lot more sense.

At Wrigley, fans are conditioned to think that the premium seats are in the bleachers. It's the place to be, the place to be seen, and the number-one destination for anyone visiting the park. Not so at Yankee Stadium. Though the Bleacher Creatures are a close bunch, the seats are nowhere near as prized as the bleachers at Wrigley. For one, Yankee Stadium doesn't sell beer in the bleachers, a fact made abundantly clear at the entrance. The seats are also not close to the field, but instead are buffered by the bullpens and Monument Park in left center field. How the hell are we supposed to hit Garret Anderson with a Duracell from here?

With Ryno's induction scheduled for the next day and with Cooperstown only a four-hour drive away, I expected to find more Cubs fans stumbling around the area. But the Cubs played here in June, and it stands to reason that most fans wouldn't return after seeing their team lose three straight.

In many ways, Yankee fans, at least the ones in the bleachers, live up to the stereotype in my Chicago mind. They're wearing unbuttoned Jeter jerseys, jean shorts and backward New Era caps. Diamond studs hang in their ears, and they say predictable things like "Yo, Jeter's my boy."

But to their credit, they're also backing up their boastful claim of baseball's best fans. The pregame roll call, where the Bleacher Creatures chant the name of every starter until acknowledged, is impressive. So is the way that everyone's hanging with every pitch. There's no frat party in the stands like at Wrigley; everyone's here to see the baseball game. That Yankee Stadium is eighty-two years old and smells like a shoe is irrelevant.

"These people aren't here for the stadium, they're not here for the bars, and they're not here to have a good time," says Joe. "They're here to watch baseball."

Then again, if the Cubs had twenty-six titles to their name and a pennant race nearly every single year, we might not make as big a deal of Wrigley Field. It'd still be a jewel, but you probably wouldn't be able to buy sweatshirts that say "Wrigley Field" instead of "Chicago Cubs." The Yankees could play in Shea Stadium and they'd still get the same type of attention.

July 31

After leaving Manhattan, Polish Joe and I stopped in a small hotel in Albany, which happened to be the only source of open rooms in the area. We were forced to share a king-sized bed, which led to my fear that a blazing fire would kill us in the middle of the night, leaving firemen and then our families to discover that we had been sleeping in the same bed. Clearly they would not have the benefit of "no room in the inn" explanations and would only be able to jump to conclusions. I briefly considered leaving a homophobic note in my car. "In case of fire, not gay."

Fortunately we awake unscathed and find a particular air of excitement for the day's festivities. Polish Joe is not a "baseball guy," but he's definitely a Cubs fan. Ryne Sandberg ranks on both of our lists of favorite all-time players, and we hit the road to Cooperstown early.

On our trip west to the National Baseball Hall of Fame, which takes us past some of the best country roads I've traveled, we discuss what made Sandberg particularly appealing to Cubs fans.

Sure, he had out-of-this-world stats for a second baseman and won the 1984 National League MVP, but there was always something that made him stand out, even though he was notorious for not saying much.

"He just seemed like he was one of us," says Polish Joe, taking a big drag off his cigarette and then hanging it out the window. "He played second base, which is a position that most anyone can play. He did the little things right, which baseball fans generally appreciate. And then he hit for power, which put him on the same level of guys like Jose Canseco and Mark McGwire. Yet those guys were superheroes. I couldn't imagine becoming like them. But imagining yourself as Ryne Sandberg was easy."

It's hard to argue. Today's induction will also see third baseman and hitting impresario Wade Boggs gain admittance into the Hall. When I was a child, my aunt Pat used to coax me to eat chicken and wild rice by explaining that she got the recipe from Boggs through a magazine article.

"Eat this and you'll hit over .300!" she would say.

I always shook my head no. As far as I was concerned, it was perfectly acceptable to be a .250 power hitter as long as it meant I could still eat Happy Meals.

We pull into downtown Cooperstown, and activity dominates Main Street. The scene looks like quintessential small-town America, if every small town had the tourist and museum money to make their Main Street look picture perfect.

At the Triple Play Café, no tables are available for breakfast, so Joe orders two egg sandwiches and eats them on the curb. My breakfast comes from the sidewalk, where VFW members are serving hot dogs, hamburgers, and sausage patties from a grill and cups of lemonade from a large orange cooler.

It's the kind of day that makes me wish my dad was here with me, so I give him a quick phone call. After a quick trip through the museum, we walk a mile south toward the field where the induction will take place. There are an estimated twenty-five to thirty thousand people here to see the two new inductees. Ryne Sandberg fans outnumber Wade Boggs supporters at an estimated three to one.

Cubs Nation has moved east, and I talk with various groups to see where they're from. Columbus, Ohio. Harrisburg, Pennsylvania. Naperville, Illinois. Gary, Indiana. The crowd is so big that we sit a ways from the stage, out past the pavilion and farther than most of those with lawn chairs.

Next to us is Tony Hutfles, a Cubs fan and recently retired air force major from San Antonio, Texas. He's on the last leg of a three-week ballpark tour, which has put five thousand miles on his F-150. He's hit nearly everything east of Texas, and he plans to hit the West Coast parks in September. When I ask him what he plans to do for a living now that he's out of the military, Hutfles answers that he's going to try to win Powerball. I laugh, thinking it's a typical response. But he mentions it again. And then five minutes later. And once more for good measure. Say this for Cubs fans, we do love a long shot.

After sitting through the inductions of Boston writer Peter Gammons, San Diego broadcaster Jerry Coleman, and Boggs, Ryno finally takes the stage to big cheers from the Cubs fans.

Chicago may not have had the most success with championships, but at least the club has had some good players. Sandberg joins Ernie Banks, Fergie Jenkins, Billy Williams, and Hack Wilson as the team's premier inductees. Everyone hopes that Ron Santo gets in while he's around to enjoy it.

Sandberg says all the right things, and the crowd breaks into applause so often that it's a State of the Union address, but for the eye-black set. Mark Grace is in the audience. So is Andre Dawson. And wouldn't you know it?

There's Ronnie Woo, up front and center.

When we least expect it, Sandberg becomes Stephen A. Douglas, launching against today's sluggers.

"A lot of people say this honor validates my career, but I didn't work hard for validation," says Sandberg, with fifty-three Hall of Famers watching from behind the lectern. "I didn't play the game right because I saw a reward at the end of the tunnel. I played it right because that's what you're supposed to do . . . play it right and with respect.

"If this validates anything, it's that learning how to bunt and hit and run and turning two is more important than knowing where to find the little red light at the dugout camera."

Cubs fans, translating the last line as a not-so-thinly-veiled barb at Sammy Sosa, go wild. If we see nothing else on this trip, it will still be worth it.

August 1

Back in May, I purchased tickets to the first game of the Baltimore–White Sox series at the Cell, thinking that the Return of Sammy to the Windy City would be a newsworthy event. But Sammy being Sammy, the slugger claimed a back injury and didn't even make the trip back home.

Today we are getting even, coming to Sammy because he wouldn't come to us. After buying $8 standing-room-only tickets, we sneak down to seats ten rows behind the Orioles dugout. Prime heckling distance.

Sosa does his part, going one for four with no homers or RBIs in a 6–3 loss to the White Sox. And we do ours.

"Hey, Sammy, we sure missed ya in Chicago!"

And because Rafael Palmeiro was suspended this morning for

steroid abuse, we ask Sammy if he knows anything about his pal Raffy.

"You guys sharing needles?"

That we are not chased from our seats by Baltimore ushers is a complete wonder. If Wrigley ushers are rottweilers, then those at Camden are poodles. Then again, it's too hot to move any-where. August in Baltimore has to be punishment for supporting a guy like Ray Lewis.

Time has not broken my reluctance to bash Sammy. When the words come out of my mouth, I do feel bad, at least a little bit. His subpar numbers this season make it a bit easier, and when I tell an Orioles fan that we're on a road trip from Chicago, he wonders if we've got room to take Sammy back to Wrigley.

If I were given the choice of season tickets in any stadium other than Wrigley, I'd think about one second and say Camden Yards. Thirteen imitators have stepped to the plate, and not one has come close to meshing new features with an old feeling as well as the park near Baltimore's Inner Harbor. The looming warehouse on Eutaw Street is the third-best feature in the majors, behind Wrigley's ivy, scoreboard and rooftops, and Fenway's Green Monster, and ahead of San Francisco's McCovey Cove and Sox Park's exploding scoreboard.

Would I take Camden over Wrigley? No, but it's closer than you think. Wide aisles, quick trips to the bathrooms, and food that doesn't taste like mush all score points. But, for some reason, time-soaked tradition wins over comfort and convenience. No matter how well you construct a neighborhood around a new ballpark, you can't fake authenticity. People walk by Wrigley all the time during games without any intention of going in. Life continues outside while forty thousand strangers stop their worlds to see eighteen men battle on a grass oasis in the middle of city life. In the new developments, that's hard to re-create. You can erect all the fancy warehouse lofts and trendy brewing companies you want and it still won't come close to a quick lap around Wrigley or Fenway.

August 2

It's hard to follow the Cubs when we're on the road. WGN Radio doesn't reach our antenna in the middle of New York and Pennsylvania, so we can't catch updates from Pat and Ron. Our only sources of information come from morning box scores in *USA Today* and *Sports Center* highlights when we reach our hotel for the night.

Just as well, because as we traipsed from Chicago to New York to Maryland, the Cubs busied themselves by losing three of four home games to the Arizona Diamondbacks. It wouldn't be July without an awful series against a team we thought was inferior. (With the wins, the D'backs, the worst team in the bigs last season, take the season series 2–5.)

Polish Joe and I power through Maryland and then 19.1 miles of the Delaware Turnpike. Philadelphia's Citizens Bank Park is in our crosshairs. The Cubs are starting a six-game road trip against the Phillies, and it'll be my first Cubs game outside of Chicago, St. Louis, and Milwaukee. When we exit our car, we find a man with a Cubs hat leaving his.

"I guess we're in this together, huh?" he says.

To my surprise, not many Cubs fans are in attendance. At least not as many as I expected. There are plenty of tickets at the window (notice I haven't written that sentence at Wrigley at all this season), and we score two cheap ones in the upper deck. Not having to haggle with scalpers? I could get used to this.

In only its second season, Citizens Bank doesn't impress much. You'd think that after three decades at Veterans Stadium, the Phillies would have learned something about Erector Set ball-parks with zero character. Yet somehow the city of Philadelphia has managed to bungle another stadium.

Yes, Philly's new park has good sightlines, comfortable seats, and easy parking. But the benefits end there. Are we at a baseball stadium? Or are we at a mall? We walk through a two-level souvenir shop seemingly dedicated to the Phillie Phanatic and it's hard to tell. Were it not for a neon Liberty Bell in right field, this park could be anywhere in the United States right now.

It raises a good question—why do Americans place a premium on quirky and distinctive baseball stadiums? We don't demand the same unique qualities in football, basketball, or hockey stadia, so why the national pastime?

We have been conditioned to expect different dimensions and features when we move from city to city. When the old ballparks were being constructed in the middle of cities, each architect had different space restrictions to work with. And as long as the bases were ninety feet apart, the designers had carte blanche with the rest of it. Football fields, basketball courts, and, to a somewhat lesser extent, hockey rinks must conform to rigid measurements that leave zero wiggle room for flair. You're not going to put a waterfall in an end zone or a giant green wall behind a basketball standard.

Baseball stadium architecture has always been about imagination and a desire to beat the Joneses across the league. It continues to be that way, and it's funny that a ballpark built in the middle of northern Chicago almost ninety years ago proves to be the standard that everyone still chases. Needless to say, when you put a stadium in the middle of an parking lot wasteland, like the Phillies did, you're not going to challenge Wrigley for top stadium dog.

For all the hype, Philly fans fail to live up to their supposed nastiness. Vicente Padilla and Carlos Zambrano are engaged in a scoreless battle through seven innings, but we see more Donovan McNabb jerseys and hear more E-A-G-L-E-S chants than cheers for the Phillies.

The Cubs take a 2–0 lead in the eighth inning on a two-run single by Aramis Ramirez. Zambrano works his way through the bottom of the eighth. The half dozen Cubs fans in our section stand and cheer as Zambrano leaves the field.

But despite the fact that Zambrano allowed only four hits over eight innings, Dusty Baker makes a call to the pen, bringing in closer Ryan Dempster for the final frame. We've already descended to the bottom level, ready to make a quick exit to Pittsburgh once the final out is official. Instead, our movement proves to be a jinx.

After forcing the first out, Dempster walks one batter . . . two batters . . . three batters, and . . . (groan) four batters.

Cubs 2, Phillies 1.

"We came all the way for this?" asks Dave, a Chicago suburbanite who has brought his eight-year-old son Brian out east on an annual baseball trip. "We could have stayed home and seen the Cubs lose at Wrigley Field. It would have been a lot cheaper."

Young Brian puts both of his hands on the brim of his Cubs hat and curls it down. It's never too early to develop an ulcer over your favorite team.

Somehow, Dempster saves us from another head-shaking Cubs loss. David Bell comes to the plate and Dempster sets him down with a strikeout. The same happens to Tomas Perez and, like that, we are headed west down I-76 with a one-game winning streak.

Having seen the Cubs win in person almost a thousand miles from home, Polish Joe declares the trip a success.

We finish our three-day sprint with trips to see the new parks in Pittsburgh, Cleveland, and Detroit. Each one impresses, especially the Pirates' PNC Park, which has all the potential for a classic fifty years down the road. But while entering an alternate universe every day is enjoyable—a trip like this brings an ever-changing roster of team colors, local legends, and furry mascots—we ultimately decide that none stacks up close to Wrigley.

"All those places were nice," says Polish Joe as we dip around Lake Michigan and back into Illinois. "But they just weren't Wrigley. I'll sacrifice the amenities for how we feel at home when we're watching the Cubs. It's hard to get a feeling like that."

Feeling warm and fuzzy toward the team inside Wrigley is another matter. After being graced by our good luck, the Cubs lose the final two in Philadelphia and then get swept by the Mets at Shea. The sweep gives the Cubs a *stellar* 0–6 record in New York this season. Heading into a three-game home set against Cincinnati, the Cubs are 54–57 and the wild card is starting to look like an improbability.

Chapter Fourteen

The Season Slides, the
Cards Hit Town (Finally),
and Cross-Dressing Comes
to the Bleachers

August 8-10—vs. Cincinnati

Coming home to Chicago does not help the Cubs. The Reds take the series opener 9–4 and the losing streak reaches six.

The hopeless slide is not a foreign feeling for a North Side fan. But after experiencing prolonged runs at the playoffs in three of the last four seasons, fighting to stay above water in August reintroduces itself painfully.

There's an Old Style campaign in Chicago that features slogans like *"Working from 9 a.m. to 1:20 p.m.? Now that's Old Style."*

I manufacture an advertising proposal in my head.

"Losing your way out of the race in August? Now that's Old Style."

Perfect.

My mind flashes back to Brian, the eight-year-old in Philadelphia who has already been trained to live with every ball thrown or hit by the Chicago Cubs. He's probably old enough to understand the game and what being a fan is like. But does he fully understand the implication? Does he realize that being a Chicago sports fan of any kind—Cubs, Sox, Bears, Bulls, and Blackhawks—requires a tolerance for an unusual amount of losing? Does he realize that we're going on four or five *generations* without a World Series title?

At some point, I may have a son of my own, and there will be a crucial decision on whether to push the Cubs on him. Then again, he'll see me in front of the television, engrossed in a game, and with hopes of pleasing me, he'll probably take it up too.

Back during the Boston series, I sat next to Christian, a young father who was taking care of his two-month-old son, Brady. When Jeromy Burnitz hit a home run onto Sheffield, Christian pointed Brady toward the field so he could see the first round-tripper of his life. This amused me, as did Brady's outfit—a Cubs onesie, a Cubs bib, and a Cubs pacifier. Born in April, the kid didn't have a chance.

"I wanted to take him to an earlier game, but it was too cold out," Christian explained to me at the time. "And so then I figured his first game should be a historic game, like the first time the Red Sox ever played in Wrigley Field."

Christian grew up a Cubs fan and now holds season tickets to Wrigley. He's been to thirty-seven stadiums and has seen the Cubs play in Puerto Rico and Japan. If there's a bigger Cubs fan, Christian doesn't know him.

I asked him about getting Brady involved with the Cubs. By having a dad with season tickets, it's possible that Brady will be bleeding red and blue before the training pants come off. My point-blank question: By pushing the Cubs, are you guilty of child abuse?

Christian laughed.

"I don't think so," he said. "I mean, the Cubs are probably going to be competitive from now on because they've got money to spend on a roster. They might not win the World Series, but they'll always have years like 1984 or two years ago. If you've got a kid and you live in a town like Pittsburgh or Milwaukee and there's no hope of a championship, as long as baseball doesn't have competitive balance, then that's a more hopeless situation."

It was a good point. With a packed stadium on eighty-one home dates, increased revenue from sources like the new dugout seats and the backing of a rich corporate owner like the Tribune Company, the Cubs have no excuse for not being in the upper echelon when it comes to salary spending. Cubs CEO Andy McPhail likes to boast that this year's payroll is $100 million, though that includes the $13 million it took for Baltimore to allow Sosa aboard their ship.

If the Cubs want to make a good-faith gesture to their fans for filling the ballpark the last three seasons, they'll boost the payroll to $120 million in the off-season in an effort to fill the holes from this year's team. That boost, though, will require a cohesive plan, something that general manager Jim Hendry didn't seem to have when entering 2005.

We need a closer? LaTroy Hawkins is just fine!

What about a left fielder?

Jason Dubois and Todd Hollandsworth aren't enough?

And then there's Dusty Baker, who has been the constant target of fan criticism since the eighth inning of game six in 2003, when he left Mark Prior to wither and flay on the mound. He's always quick to play the race card or invent a spectacular new way to place the blame on someone (or something) other than himself or his players.

Favorite Dustyisms: Steve Stone was the sole source of the Cubs' collapse in 2004. Black players are better than whites when they're playing in hot weather. Free agents won't want to come to Wrigley because we mercilessly booed Hawkins when he was here.

Baker is quickly wearing thin with Cubs fans, who are tired of seeing a team play without any sense of consistency, urgency, or accountability. During the last homestand, I saw a man wearing an "In Dusty We Trusty" shirt that was popular during the 2003 playoffs. A thick black marker line was drawn through each word.

On Tuesday afternoon, the Cubs continue their losing streak, dropping a game to the Reds 8–3 and falling seven games behind Houston in the wild-card race. The team's record of five games below .500 is the low point of the season.

At least until Wednesday afternoon's series ender. I scam a ticket for $10 and hang in the standing-room-only space behind the terrace level. Rookie Rich Hill is starting, and when the fourth inning comes around, he shows his young age. Hill surrenders a home run to Ryan Freel to give Cincinnati a 1–0 lead. Then, after loading the bases, Hill walks not one but two batters, the second being Reds pitcher Eric Milton. Reliever Michael Wuertz doesn't do a much better job, and by the end of the inning the Reds are leading 7–0. The Cubs are on their way to their second eight-game losing streak of the season (in addition to the separate seven-game skid at the start of May).

Between innings, an elderly African-American usher stops to wipe his brow with his cap. He looks at me and manages a chuckle.

"I'm dying out here," he says, trying to catch a break behind a pillar, where his boss won't see him. "Just like the Cubs."

A female paramedic walks by and they share smiles.

"If I was at home, I'd turn this off and go do something else," she tells the usher. "But here there's nothing I can do about it."

On the television monitors, WGN is showing a young girl holding a sign. It says "Dear Cubs, Please Stop Losing."

A beer vendor walks up the aisle yelling, "Sorrow beer! Get your sorrow beer! It's good for helping you forget!"

On the radio, Pat Hughes is helping console a downtrodden Ron Santo by using an old Cubs broadcasting diversion for when the team's not playing well. He turns his attention toward Lake Michigan, which can easily be seen from the upper deck.

"Lake Michigan is a beautiful shade of blue," Hughes says. "I don't see any sailboats out there, though. Do you, Ronnie?"

I head outside and call it a day. I'd rather hang with the Ballhawks on the corner than watch the team flail through another nine innings. (The Cubs will lose by a final score of 8–2.)

When I reach the corner, Moe Mullins and Dave Davison are the corner's lone occupants. Everyone else has something to do today. Mullins and Davison are resting in lawn chairs, near the fire hydrant, which has again been painted purple. A local woman with a penchant for Northwestern is rumored to be the culprit. Davison heads to the Waveland firehouse and asks if I want something to drink from the vending machine. It's like I'm a guest in his home, and, in a way, I am.

Mullins remains in his chair, a copy of the *Sun-Times* on the cement below his feet. The number of afternoons he's spent out here is staggering to comprehend and I feel a bit foolish even acting like I know a tenth as much about the neighborhood as he does.

"I bet all this losing in August feels familiar," I say.

"It's the same thing as always," says Mullins, half listening to his radio headphones. "The main difference is that people are still coming out to watch. Look at how full that ballpark is right now. They used to close the upper deck because no one was coming out here."

Mullins grew up in a house just down Kenmore. His family sold it in the late '60s for under forty thousand dollars. He stops to laugh when he thinks about how much it would be sold for now.

"Nobody wanted to live here thirty years ago," Mullins says. "You had the Latin Eagles [gang] running all over the place. It wasn't a nice place to be. I think some people don't realize that."

In the late innings, Howard, a Wrigley beer vendor who also

sells T-shirts around the park after the games, joins us. Howard heads to his car, which is parked on Kenmore and contains a small cooler of beer. He comes back to the corner, cracks a can and starts drinking.

When he thinks about the upcoming weekend, Howard is particularly pleased. The Cardinals are hitting Wrigley for the first time this season, and he has a large stock of "St. Louis Sucks" T-shirts that he's certain will sell well. In fact, he's going to peddle the shirts after this game, for any fans that may want to come prepared for the four-game series.

"You see all these big souvenir stands and shops around here and all of them are making money," he says. "I'm just a man with a bag who wants a piece of that action."

After about ten minutes, Howard heads back to the cooler in his car. He is greeted by a Chicago police officer when he returns.

Busted for public consumption?

Not quite.

"Hey! How ya doing?" Howard yells down the street to the officer, who happens to be a longtime friend. "Hey, you need a beer?"

"C'mon, Howard, I'm on duty," says the officer.

"You can have just one!"

"No, I can't."

"Well, can I have yours for you?"

"Be my guest."

With that, Howard heads back to his car.

"One more," he says.

August 11–14—vs. St. Louis

On Friday afternoon, the day after the Cubs end their losing streak with an 11–4 romp over the Cardinals, I see Howard selling beer in the upper deck in left field. I ask him how the T-shirt business is going. There's some stiff competition out there for this four-game series. Before yesterday's game, a couple of young guys were hawking T-shirts that read "Cardinals Fans Take It in Their Pujols," a rough reference to St. Louis star Albert Pujols (pronounced, as any third-grader will say with a nervous giggle, "poo-holes").

"Going pretty well," says Howard, sweating and trudging up the steps for another sale before he can spit out a longer response.

The vendors are the unsung heroes of Wrigley Field, armed with any combination of beer, soda, peanuts, hot dogs, and malt cups. Since I haven't sat in the same spot more than once (beer vendors in the bleachers are not allowed), I haven't become chummy with any single vendor. Instead, I recognize—and most fans probably do the same thing—each vendor by a particular characteristic or quirk.

There's the beer vendor who looks like a skinnier version of Scottie Pippen. And the guy we call the Champ because he looks like Apollo Creed, only with about a hundred more pounds of muscle.

There's the scrawny old man who sells malt cups with a sad and bewildered look on his face. And the hot dog vendor whose cry is so eardrum-piercingly loud that I once almost challenged him to a fight in the upper deck of the United Center. On a quiet day at Sox Park, his cries can dominate the radio and television broadcasts from the South Side.

My favorite, though, is the guy who sells hot dogs in the bleachers. He doesn't come around often, but when he does, he sets up shop in the aisle, scans the crowd, and lets forth with the best pitch in Wrigley.

Hot dogs! . . . Hot dogs!

Then, kicking it into gear with a L'il John guttural shout:

Haahhhhhttt Digggggggggitttty Duhhhawwwwwgs!

And then back to normal.

Hot dogs!

But I really don't have that much interaction with the vendors. The best-kept secret about Wrigley Field is that you can bring in any type of food or drink you want, so long as it isn't a six-pack of beer or a pint of Jack Daniel's.* Because the food at Wrigley is overpriced and frankly not very good, I almost always stop at 7-Eleven for a bottle of water and a bag of Cracker Jack. Or at Jimmy John's for a No. 2—the delectable Turkey Tom. Or at McDonald's for the two cheeseburger meal.

I am a very healthy eater.

Today is Taco Bell day, and for the price of a three hardshell taco combo meal, Dan the college friend has given me a $42 seat in the upper deck. A girl eyes my quesadilla as we rip open tiny packets of fire sauce.

"You can bring that inside?" she asks, her eyes wide. "I had no idea."

After yesterday's game, the Cubs hold a 4–2 edge in the season series over the Cardinals. It doesn't matter much, though, because St. Louis owns an insurmountable lead in the NL Central. At 73–43, the Cardinals are seventeen games ahead of the Cubs in the standings.

It's a similar situation to last season, when the Cardinals sped away from the division by mid-July. The two teams finished playing their head-to-head games by July 20, and Cubs fans bemoaned the lack of late-season opportunities against the Cards. This year, the two teams play most of their games over the final two months of the season, and guess what? It doesn't matter again.

The Wrigley crowd is still an enthusiastic one, especially con-

---

Here's another loophole—a half pint of rum dumped into a Big Gulp from the 7-Eleven almost always gets through the gates as well. You will see any number of people mixing them up just before game time on the corner of Sheffield.

sidering that a good showing against the Cardinals could provide some resuscitation in the wild-card race. Yes, we still have hope, even after the second eight-game losing streak of the season.

For sheer intensity and pageantry, the Cubs-Cardinals series ranks only behind Yankees–Red Sox. When St. Louis comes to Wrigley, it seems as if half of Missouri comes with them. Cardinals' red is the only team color to stand out among the blue-clad faithful at Wrigley, and the fans' cheers can often be louder than when the White Sox come to visit.

In our section alone, I would estimate that 30 percent of the fans are here for the Cardinals. And while Cubs fans hate the Redbirds with a passion, the interaction between the two groups is almost always civil. There are good-natured barbs, sure, but none of the testosterone-fueled rage we saw toward Red Sox fans at Yankee Stadium.

The relationship between Cubs and Cardinals fans is hard to describe. From an egotistical Cubs fan perspective, it doesn't seem like the Cards have an edge over us. But from a historical standpoint, they do. The Cardinals are what the Cubs would like to be: an almost perennial contender and arguably the top franchise in the National League. The Cardinals have nine World Series titles to their name, but, as we like to point out, the last one came early in the Reagan administration.

Also, the Cardinals have fleeced the Cubs in arguably the most lopsided trade in history (Ernie Broglio for Lou Brock), have a genius in Tony LaRussa for a manager (Cubs fans will vehemently argue this point), and a franchise cornerstone in Pujols.

So how do Cubs fans counter the Cardinals' apparent superiority? By making the following claims:

1. We don't play in the bland batting donut that is Busch Stadium (a jab that will be rendered ineffective with the Cards' new stadium in 2006).

2. The Brock trade was nullified by our eventual acquisition of Harry Caray, who in turn made the Cubs more popular worldwide than the Cardinals could ever hope to be.

3. We don't have to live in the general armpit that is the greater St. Louis metropolitan area. I'm serious about this. Not even writing a book about the Cubs could bring me to visit St. Louis.

At any rate, the Cubs come through with another unlikely victory, winning 4–1 to give us fans a little more ammunition in Friday night bar arguments. The win marks the first two-game winning streak in almost three weeks for the Cubs.

When it comes to the Cubs Internet message boards, I'm a habitual lurker. There's a certain thrill in ascertaining that there are fans who share the same views after a big win or a big loss. It's also amusing to find the couple of crackpots out there who have worked out a six-team trade where the Cubs can trade Jose Macias for Brian Giles, Billy Wagner and Roy Halladay.

On some of the message boards, the hometown of each poster is listed. Not surprisingly, many of the members follow the Cubs from around the world. From Salt Lake City, Utah, to an aircraft carrier in the middle of the Persian Gulf, there are countless numbers of fans who overcome logistical challenges to follow the team through cable television, Internet broadcasts, and satellite radio.

When I lived in Kansas City, it was hard enough to keep track of the Cubs from five hundred miles away. Yet I never had room to complain.

In the middle of 2003, one of my best friends from high school, Jonathan, announced that he was joining the Peace Corps and heading to Mongolia for a two-year service period. This came as quite a shock to everyone, seeing as how none of us was the type to sleep in huts or drink vodka made from fermented goat's milk.

And yet Jonathan, who was one of my constant companions at Wrigley during our high school and college years, seemed sure of his decision. But one thing made him nervous . . . the Cubs' pitching was just beginning to gel and a run at the NL Central looked like a possibility.

On the night we said our good-byes, Jonathan made a prediction.

"Just watch," he said. "I'm going to move to Mongolia and the Cubs are going to win the World Series. It's going to take something like me moving to the outer reaches of nowhere for the Cubs to make it."

So Jonathan made a pledge. If the Cubs reached the World Series, he would buy a plane ticket and fly back to Chicago. This presented a problem, because Jonathan would need to actually *find out* that the Cubs qualified for the playoffs and made it through to the final frame. Considering he would be living in the Mongolian countryside, monitoring the situation would be no small feat without electricity or cell phones.

On almost every day of September 2003, Jonathan either walked or found a ride into the nearest city, where a slow Internet connection awaited. Each day, he'd log in and check the standings on Yahoo! Sports. If he timed it right, he could catch a few innings of the Internet broadcast, where small numbers and icons brought him the situation live from Wrigley, on the other side of the world.

We exchanged e-mails throughout the pennant chase, and again when the Cubs beat the Braves for their first postseason series win since 1908. Job obligations kept him away from the computer for most of the series with the Marlins, but when he finally checked his messages, there was one waiting from his mother.

"Dear Jonathan," it read. "The Cubs are up three games to one on the Florida Fish (sic) and are going to the World Series! When should I book your plane ticket so you can come home?"

The message was the equivalent of a punch to the stomach for Jonathan.

"It was then I knew that the Cubs were going to blow it," he wrote to me later. "There was no question about it."

Jonathan followed the Cubs' collapse in 2004 and watched as the team got off to this season's less-than-stellar start. In April, I asked him if he'd like to share his experiences of being a Cub fan in a distant land. No problem, he said.

"I've actually got enough Cubs clothing here to outfit a Little League team," he wrote. "If you need a picture of an old woman milking a yak in a Cubs jersey or a hot young Mongol flashing her tits while riding a camel and wearing a Cubs hat, just let me know."

In early July, he told me his time was up and he would be back in Chicago by early August. A friend had bought him bleacher tickets for the Saturday game against the Cardinals. I told him we'd throw him a welcome home party, so long as he brought the pictures of that hot young Mongol.

Saturday's game against the Cardinals is delayed by a steady shower of rain, so our group, which includes a stateside Jonathan and my friend Renee from Madison, forms a huddle in the middle of the Cubby Bear. We set to work on a few rounds in plastic cups.

"What are the bars like in Mongolia?" I ask Jonathan.

"They're a lot like the Cubby Bear," he says. "Only with less big-screen televisions and more Cardinals fans."

Rain delays happen to be a main ingredient for a good Saturday in the Wrigley Field bleachers. Everyone stays in the bars until the game starts, so the opportunity for quick inebriation is extended. Some people inevitably give up and head home, so cheap tickets are easier to find on the street and the stands are less crowded, leading to more drunken fun among those still present.

My point is proven when the game finally begins an hour and a half later than originally scheduled. Outside the bleacher entrance, two Cardinals fans wearing Afro wigs are being arrested on Sheffield. The packed patio at Murphy's is applauding the work of the police officers. The two fans are wearing shirts that say "Cubs-19" and "Suck-08." The cops are holding the fans in reverse order, so the message is reversed. I can't help but wonder if it's a coincidence.

Minutes later, in the right field bleachers, I get blindsided by a blur of pink-shirted muscle. Someone behind me is holding my shoulders. He is thrusting his pelvis into my ass while another man comes 'round front, dodges my swipes, grabs my hips, and starts grinding, Christina Aguilera style.

The men are laughing and someone is taking pictures. I finally break free and jump up two bleacher rows to safety.

"What the . . . ?"

"Hey, man, we're just having some fun," says a man who will later introduce himself as Eddie. "We didn't mean anything by it."

Everyone around me is laughing, and Eddie's compatriot, John, has already moved to rubbing up on Renee. Both Eddie and John are wearing pink Cubs T-shirts made for women. The tags say "Large," but they are ill-fitting.

"We walked out of the Cubby Bear and saw these shirts so we bought them," Eddie says. "I know they look pretty gay, but it's helping us to get chicks. Two girls just flashed us on the way in here."

I tell Eddie that Wrigley Field is only a few blocks from Boys Town, an area where a large portion of Chicago's gay population lives.* Eddie just shrugs.†

"So?"

Eddie and John are from Philadelphia, and they're in town celebrating John's recent divorce. It has been a successful trip, says Eddie, because John hooked up with a girl last night. Unfortunately, she was staying out near the airport, and when John made his escape, he had no idea where he was.

The presence of Eddie and John reinforces my idea that people make their way to Wrigley Field to find something they can't have elsewhere. Eddie affirms my belief.

"You can't do this sort of thing at a baseball game in Philadelphia," he says, and we both look over at John, who has put his arm around Renee. "I used to go sit in the Vet as a kid and throw super bouncy balls at the opposing outfielders. [Wrigley] is about baseball, dude. All the other stuff that comes with it is just a bonus."

That baseball is being played on the field comes as news to all of us as we drink a few more beers, yell insults at Cardinals outfielder Jim Edmonds, and get ready for an all-night barbecue at my house. John entertains himself by grabbing a Cardinals T-shirt from another friend, ripping it to pieces, and making himself a bra from one of the sleeves. Bleacher security keeps a close eye on John but retreats once they realize that he is only entertaining everyone. It beats what's happening on the field, as Chris Carpenter, a Cy Young candidate, defeats the Cubs 5–2 to end Chicago's nascent winning streak.

---

*The best-selling T-shirt on the South Side reads, "Wrigley Field: World's Largest Gay Bar."
†At this point, I tell him my favorite Cubs joke. Q: How many gay guys does it take to flip over a car and set it on fire? A: We'll find out when the Cubs win the World Series.

I look over at Jonathan, who is having a great time being back at the place he thought about many times during the cold Mongolian winters. After two years of horse racing and a Mongolian sport so ridiculous that the particulars are easily forgotten, baseball is again filling the primal need of a kid from Chicagoland.

Chapter Fifteen

On the Latin Eagles,
Ryno Has Another
Day in the Sun,
and Stumbling Toward
September

August 22-24—vs. Atlanta

When we reach my spot, third row in the bleachers, we find it has been taken over by an outing from a brokerage house or a law firm or something. I'm too put off to find out exactly where they've come from.

Instead, we sit in the second row and there's ten feet of empty bench on either side of us. I'm at the game with Chris, who has just returned from D.C. after serving as a summer associate in a high-octane law firm. In typical wine-and-dine fashion, she was taken to skyboxes at Camden Yards and RFK, fed crab cakes and pints of summer ale, and ushered in and out of special entrances. How the other half lives, I tell her.

Today, on a Tuesday night, she's back among the scrubs in the bleachers, sipping from a water bottle and eating $3.25 hot dogs that only look appetizing to Dobermans.

"It's much different down here," she says.

After winning against St. Louis on Sunday, the Cubs left town for a six-game road trip to Houston and Colorado. The team went 3–3 over that stretch, but dropped two of three to the Rockies, an inexcusable failure against the league's worst team.

The Cubs returned home last night and opened a three-game

series against Atlanta with a 4–2 loss by way of a two-run homer by Chipper Jones off new reliever Kerry Wood in the ninth inning. The Cubs are now six and a half games out of the wild-card race with six teams in front of them.

The smart money has been on the Cubs not making the playoffs. For quite some time. The team's inconsistency and lack of heart were identified early on and thus our hopes never soared too high. But the National League has only two good teams—St. Louis and Atlanta—so the mediocre middle has left the door slightly open.

Now, for the first time, it seems entirely shut. It's unseasonably cool for a late August night, and Wrigley is only a third full by the time of the first pitch by starter Jerome Williams. When the Cubs took the field, there was only a halfhearted round of applause. Jeromy Burnitz took his place in right field and only a few bleacherites could be bothered to greet him with encouragement.

Crowd attitude meter: *What's the point?*

Outside the stadium, the scalpers are taking a pounding and I mark August 23 as my first big victory over "Bleacher Bob," the alpha ticket dealer on the corner by Murphy's.

The takedown went like this: A half hour before the game, we run into Bob walking north on Sheffield. He starts by offering bleachers for $30 apiece. I balk and keep on walking. Bob counters with an offer of $20 apiece, essentially giving us a two-for-one ticket deal. Though I know he's still making money off the sale (otherwise he wouldn't be dumping this early), it seems fair and I agree. Wanting to know a little more about the street scalping business, I wonder if Bleacher Bob will ever clue me in on his secrets. Finally I ask him, point-blank.

"So, Bob, when do you want to sit down and chat?"

He shrugs. "Scalpers are like doctors and lawyers," he says. "Everyone wants to talk with us."

"So when is a good time?"

"I don't need any publicity."

"Do you make a lot of money?"

"I'm still doing it, aren't I?"

"How long have you been doing this?"

"Twenty years."

"How you doing moneywise this year?"

"Everything was going great. And then the Cubs decided to take their season and flush it down the toilet. Now I can't get anything for these tickets."

The Wrigleyville scalpers have acted like this toward me all season. At first, they were eager to set the record straight, and tell me why they're providing such a valuable service to the citizens of Chicago, so they initially agreed to an interview. But then when go-time came, they pretended to forget who I was or, like our friend today, say they don't need any publicity. Other than the IRS, I'm not sure what they're afraid of. Maybe they know scalping isn't a very honorable way to make a living. Maybe they know they're one level above the guys who pelt my e-mail inbox with penis enlargement spam.

Bleacher Bob, though, is okay with me, but I'm not sure why. After shaking my hand, he heads back to his spot near Murphy's, trying to dump the stack of tickets in his hand. There are deals to be had, folks.

The Cubs strike with four runs in the bottom of the third, including a bases-loaded walk drawn by our man in right field, Burnitz. In the next inning, Burnitz comes up in the same situation. Sacks packed. Facing Atlanta's Joey Devine, Burnitz lifts a drive that lands in the center field bushes. Cubs lead 8–0.

When Burnitz takes right field in the top of the fifth, he's greeted with more enthusiasm than at the start. He tips his cap, revealing his bald head and more of his square-jaw profile. He looks a little like Popeye, or maybe, more accurately, like one of those goons from *Popeye*.

The atmosphere loosens up a bit with the Cubs on their way to a 10–1 victory. The work group behind us sits and heckles Atlanta's super-rookie right fielder, Jeff Francoeur, who's only been in the majors for thirty-four games. He provides an easy target— just *how* do you pronounce that last name?

Francoeur, all of twenty-one years old, responds by shooting us bemused grins between pitches, holding his hand to his ear on misheard heckles, and furnishing a spot-on Sosa imitation, complete with heart taps and blown kisses. Cincinnati's Austin Kearns acts the same way. The players are so cute when they're young. Yet when they get older and Wrigley Field is no longer a novelty and baseball has become a job, they will change. Not even Burnitz really pays us that much attention.

In the fourth inning, a Hispanic man in his mid-thirties and his young son join us. The man is wearing carpenter jeans, a cellphone holster, and several gaudy gold rings. His son has a Cubs hat that features at least twelve logos and is taking pictures on his cell phone camera.

"I used to live in one of those buildings over there on Sheffield," volunteers the man, whose name is Edwin. "Lived there in a one-bedroom with my parents and my brother. Rent was $350 a month."

While a majority of Cubs fans are lily white, there's a large contingent of Hispanic fans. That's because, as mentioned before, Wrigleyville used to be home for a large Hispanic population. And even though part of the crowd has been priced out of the neighborhood and has moved west down Irving Park Road, they remain loyal.

Interested in what life in Wrigleyville was like back then, I prod Edwin for further details about the gang activity that used to rule in the area.

"The Latin Eagles owned all of this down here," says Edwin.

"I used to run with those guys. But gangs, man, they're the worst things that have ever been invented."

Was it dangerous for Cubs fans?

"Nah, man, we left the Cubs fans alone," Edwin says. "Maybe broke into their cars or something. We were too busy fighting the other gangs. The Stones were coming in from the south and the LKs were coming in from the north. We had to fight off both sides; we didn't have time for anything else."

You can still find some of the Eagles running around, Edwin says, but drug addictions and jail time took down most of the organization's top guys. All the gang activity has mostly shifted north and west of Wrigleyville. "Fancy rich folks," as Edwin puts it, aren't much for gangs in their neighborhood.

But that's all behind him, Edwin says before continuing to emphasize, for the benefit of his son, how bad gangs are. Now his only rivalry comes on the scoreboard. Edwin busies himself with watching the score of the White Sox–Minnesota game, where Sox pitcher Freddy Garcia is about to *lose* a one-hit game, 1–0, to the Twins. The Sox have lost eight of their last nine games, seeing a big chunk of their AL Central lead disappear in the process.

"I can't have the Sox winning, man," he says. "I got a brother-in-law down there on the South Side. I'll never hear the end of it."

August 26-28—vs. Florida
August 29-31—vs. Los Angeles

Two straight losses open the series with Florida, and the grind toward the season's final day is officially on. By falling to seven games under .500, the Cubs have officially smothered any outside chance they had at making the playoffs.

Still the fans come out. This is what happens when a team sells out a season before the first pitch is even thrown. Because the tickets are so expensive, no one wants to stay home and eat the cost. So they soldier on, come out to the park and have a good time, even if the Cubs aren't very good. It's something Chicagoans have had a lot of practice with.

To date, I would venture that the Cubs' biggest days were the first two games of the Boston series, when the team powered its way to victories over the defending World Series champions. The second would be July 30, when Ryne Sandberg entered the Hall of Fame, and the third would be today, a Sunday, when the Cubs officially retire Ryno's number 23.

Wrigley is almost full forty-five minutes before game time, and the weather is everything you would hope from a Sunday afternoon in late summer. "Ryne Sandberg: Second to None," reads a giant sign on the left field fence in the bleachers, and five trumpeters announce the start of the ceremony. Members of the Cubs' top triumvirate—Ernie Banks, Ron Santo, and Billy Williams—take their seats.

Sandberg enters to a standing ovation, holding his wife Margaret's hand. His children and stepchildren are already seated and it's impossible not to imagine what his stepchildren must have been thinking once he started dating Margaret.

"Hey, who's the new guy your mom is dating?"

"Ryne Sandberg."

"No, really, who?"

Sandberg gives an abbreviated speech, touching on a couple of topics but getting nowhere near as in-depth as his excellent Hall of Fame address. A man in the terrace reserve yells, "We love you, Ryno!" causing Sandberg to pause. "I love you, too," he yells back.

The day couldn't rank much higher on the sugary sweet meter, but no one seems to mind. After the number flag is raised up the right field pole, Ryne and Margaret make a trip around the park, and each section rises to its feet as they pass. Someone in the left field bleachers tosses a baseball to Sandberg and he tosses it back with ease.

"I wonder if he can start at second today," says a man behind me.

"Maybe he can lead off too," his friend says.

For a few minutes at least, we are transported back to 1984: The Cubs are in the middle of a magical season and Sandberg is on his way to the NL MVP.

Throughout the game, Sandberg emerges on the catwalk behind the skyboxes, drawing applause from those in the terrace reserved whenever he does. Perhaps inspired by the presence of Cubs royalty, the team puts on an exhibition, riding an offensive explosion to a 14–3 victory.

On the walk home, the feeling in my head is happy and content. A Sunday at Wrigley turned out to be worth the price of admission. Since Dan the college friend gave me today's ticket, I only had to buy him two sandwiches and a giant pickle from Jimmy John's in return. It's the deal of the season.

September

Q: *Any leftover stories from the road trip you took?*
A: Oh, do I have stories. You could start with us leaving Yankee Stadium early because of a dinner date, only to find out on the turnpike six hours later that the Yankees had staged a late-inning comeback win. Or how about our arrival in Pittsburgh, when a tollbooth worker called us both "dickheads" because we jokingly complained about the $11 toll? Our biggest mishap came near PNC Park when Polish Joe locked the keys in the 'Stanger, an act that forced him to wait for Triple-A and miss most of the game.

But my favorite tale comes from Cleveland, when I spent an afternoon writing in the hotel room while Joe went out to "see the city." As far as I can tell, this only entailed visiting a strip club, because when he got back, he was gung-ho about visiting a club after the Indians game. Two dancers had told Joe they would meet him there.

Eight hours later, I was in a Coyote Ugly knockoff bar, watching Joe ride a mechanical bull while a former member of Warrant covered rock songs from the '80s. The strippers never showed, and when we left, Joe was left saying, "I can't believe they didn't meet us here."

"You're right," I said. "Strippers are usually very trustworthy."

Q: *You saw some good baseball games on the trip (four of the six games were decided in the final two innings). After* *that, are you tired of watching the wildly inconsistent Cubs?*

A: I guess you could say that, though I try to remind myself that a bad day at the ballpark is better than the best day in a cubicle. (Someone must have surely said that before, though attribution has been hard to find.) Still, this year's version of the Cubs don't play my ideal brand of baseball. Without a true leadoff hitter, they don't play station-to-station baseball, instead waiting for Derrek Lee, Aramis Ramirez, or Jeromy Burnitz to club a three-run home run. It's a recipe for disaster and particularly distasteful for someone like myself. A 2–1 pitchers' duel that ends on a sac fly can be better than Cherry Vanilla Dr Pepper (and yes, that is saying something).

Q: *Who's been going to all these games with you?*

A: Anybody who can stomach it, really. At this point, I'd like to mention my friend Will Byington, whom I met back in May. Will lives across the street from Wrigley in the rooftop building that I was ejected from earlier this season. After the games, he sells his original photography of the stadium from the fence outside his apartment. Or at least he used to. Someone complained to the alderman and Will was forced to stop. Now he sells his pictures over the Internet and to businesses around the park. The reason that Will and I are friends is that we're remarkably similar. He used to be a merchandise manager for Cowboy Mouth, a New Orleans–based band. He left that job and moved to Wrigleyville so that he could attend as many Cubs games as possible. As such, he's often the only one around when game time comes and I've got an extra ticket. Our only differences can be found in our respective outlooks. While I've maintained that the Cubs are dead in the water, Will says he's a believer until the end. He wants to see the elimination number fall to zero before he packs it all in.

Q: *Now that the Cubs' season is effectively over, is there anything worth seeing in September? Or will you pack it in early?*

A: Not a chance. The month of September will be an interesting one at Wrigley, even if it's not about the baseball the Cubs are playing. Jimmy Buffett is playing Wrigley over Labor Day weekend, the first (and possibly last) stand-alone concert played in the park. The Cardinals come to town for another four-game series. And there's a good chance I'll die of a hot dog–induced heart attack or that my liver will call it quits somewhere between the Cubby Bear and the Full Shilling. It should make for quite a finish.

Chapter Sixteen

Marga Wrigleyville, the Icons, and the Start of Bears Season

September 4–5—Jimmy Buffett

Fenway Park gets the Rolling Stones. We get Jimmy Buffett.

It seems appropriate. The most consistent and heavy hitters in the history of rock and roll will be playing in the home of the reigning World Series champions. Meanwhile, Jimmy Buffett, who at some point must have figured out that his music wasn't very good but might be tolerable if his fans were shit-faced and wearing Hawaiian shirts, is playing at Wrigley Field, home of a team that established the market on style over substance.

I'm getting ahead of myself here, especially considering that I've never actually been to a Jimmy Buffett concert, and, for all I know, it could be better than a bathtub full of banana pudding.

That Buffett is even playing two shows at Wrigley Field is a wonder in itself. Mr. Tropical first approached the Cubs about playing at the stadium almost ten years ago, and it has taken this long for the team to finally agree.

The deciding factor, of course, was money. With tickets priced at $140 and $90, Buffett sold out two shows with relative ease. The concerts were an easy decision, team officials say, because Buffett is a guaranteed sellout and plays music that is acceptable for the neighborhood. Apparently the Cubs are convinced the Hell's Angels are still providing security for the Rolling Stones.

The concert marks the first time a stand-alone artist has played an event at Wrigley Field. In order to get a blessing from Alderman Tom Tunney, the Cubs had to agree they wouldn't hold any concerts in 2006 and would set a number of tickets aside for neighborhood residents, and both Buffett and the team made several donations to charitable causes around Wrigleyville.

(When you follow the happenings in the neighborhood, you quickly learn that there are residents opposed to *anything* ever happening at Wrigley Field. If they had it their way, the Cubs would play all their games on the road, leaving the parking and silence to themselves. All of which raises the question, why the hell did you move to Wrigleyville if you don't like the noise or the crowds?)

While I would have preferred to see the Rolling Stones or Pearl Jam or a Smashing Pumpkins reunion (both Eddie Vedder and Billy Corgan are big Cubs fans), I ultimately decide that Buffett deserves to be given a chance.

For two days, that is exactly what I do.

Will throws a party for Sunday night's concert at his apartment on Sheffield. The shelves at the Osco on Southport are picked clean of Captain Morgan, so I bring a few bottles of ready-made mudslide mix, quickly commandeer Will's blender and start mixing for the ladies. The apartment soon fills up, and while we cannot hear the concert from inside, it doesn't matter much. A redhead wearing tight green pants and a straw hat becomes everyone's favorite hit-on target. A man wanders off the street and into the party wearing an "I (heart) lesbians" T-shirt. His torso is covered in what we think is a mixture of beer, sweat, and margarita mix. My buddy Soks shows, and it turns out we both know the same people. Small world.

The view from Will's window is remarkable. The upper grandstand is bathed in a bluish light and the people inside are a continuous moving mass, moving and swaying to the music. The whole thing looks like a Phish concert for people who like shopping at Tommy Bahama.

We bring our drinks down to the stoop on Sheffield and watch two muscle-bound guys pummel each other. It takes a while for the police to respond, and by the time they do, one of the men is gone. An officer tells me not to bring my drink out onto the sidewalk. They're not making arrests for public consumption—how could they?—but please, try and police yourselves, he says.

The bleachers are empty because the large stage is set in center field. At the end of the show, Buffett retires to the last row in the right field bleachers, in the very same spot I sat in late April. A spotlight shines from the upper deck. Buffett sits with a partner. Both play acoustic guitars. The song is "City of New Orleans," the classic folk song by Steve Goodman, the creator of "Go Cubs Go." In the past week, Hurricane Katrina has decimated New Orleans, so, considering the circumstances, the Chicago crowd goes wild when Buffett plays the song by his late friend.

When the song is done, Buffett raises his guitar into the air with one hand and heads backstage. The crowd in Wrigley screams for an encore, but we've seen enough and head back upstairs. Our party is only beginning.

September 12–14—vs. Cincinnati

If I didn't have a pocket schedule, I could have sworn that the Reds are visiting Wrigley for the twelfth time this season. The schedule says Cincinnati has only been here three times, but watching the free-swinging antics of Adam Dunn and Austin Kearns can wear on your soul. Thank God I'm not a Reds fan.

The Cubs have worked their way into an interesting spot. With the pressure off, the team just finished an 8–2 road trip, which included a sweep in Pittsburgh, two wins in St. Louis, and three wins in San Francisco. The pro-Cubs media again seems to think the wild card is a possibility, even though the margin is still five games and the Cubs would have to get by the Astros, Phillies, Nationals, and Marlins in the final three weeks of the season to do so. I'm all for the perpetual hope of the Chicago fan, but this is getting a bit ridiculous. Just because you're a Cubs fan doesn't mean you should ignore things like a weak bullpen, no decent players in the first or second spots, or a manager like Dusty Baker, who happens to be completely lost when it comes to developing young talent.

The gullible don't get to believe for long. The Cubs drop a 5–2 decision on Monday night and we're back to the usual version of this year's team, the one that refuses to get a win when it needs it the most.

We are left with two bottom-feeders playing out the string in front of another sellout crowd. The talk around the bleachers varies. I spend a good amount of time during Monday night's game breaking down the debut of the Bears, a 9–7 loss in Washington.

Around here, it's Bears season, and when not talking about the Monsters of the Midway, we are talking about our fantasy football teams or our allegiances toward our alma maters.

Fall is a funny time because both Cubs and Sox fans come together to support the Bears. When you're sitting in the stands at Soldier Field, no distinction is made between the two camps. As for college football season, the Wrigley proletariat breaks up and heads different ways and wears different colors on Saturdays. Will's Northwoods Inn is a Wisconsin bar. The Green Mill is for Spartan backers. McGee's plays host to Notre Dame and Nebraska grads. All the recent college grads will reunite once the next Cubs season begins.

Lately I've been noticing the signage in the bars and shops around Wrigleyville. Everything seems to promise that "Next Year Is Here" or claim "Our Year, Our Beer." Now it seems silly, like the propaganda of an empire that never held a coronation ceremony.

I've been doing a lot of thinking and apart from the performances, the season has been great. Everyone should get a summer off to experience a stint in Wrigley Field. No obligations except for showing up at (or around) 1:20 p.m.

Yet something always seemed to be missing, and I only recently put my finger on it. I've mentioned Harry Caray more than a couple times in passing, but I haven't taken the time to expound on what he continues to mean around these parts.

Seven years after his death, I don't think we've fully accepted that he's gone and not coming back. His statue greets everyone outside, and the famous silhouette rests above the press box. But it's not the same.

When Harry was here, he was the lifeblood of the party scene, the behemoth who took a losing team and its quaint old stadium and elevated both to sports and pop culture icons using nothing more than simple enthusiasm and love. If the Cubs were a baseball version of the Galactic Empire in *Star Wars*, then Harry was its emperor, controlling the moods of Cubs Nation through his seventh-inning stretch and frenetic home run calls.

"It might be . . . It could be . . . It is!"

Harry died in 1998, right before the beginning of spring training, and I remember, seeing the news on WGN while sitting in my college dorm room, I actually cried. He was a holdover from my youth, a hero in the city of Chicago, and a third grandfather to most of us who tuned in to listen.

In the years since his death, the Tribune Company has done any number of things to keep his memory alive, but it all seems so commercial and bottom-line oriented. When NASCAR star

Jeff Gordon climbs into the booth and yells, "Welcome to Wrigley Stadium," that's not a celebration and that's not cute and it's not an honor to Harry. It's a blatant ploy to sell Pepsi or paint or whatever Gordo is pushing that day. True fans have called for the end of the "celebrity" singers in the seventh inning, but the "tradition" has continued, giving the chance for *Desperate Housewives* cast members to plug their show.

This is a hypocritical view, considering that Harry was the ultimate pitchman and pushed Budweiser beer as if the six-packs weren't moving off the shelves. But there was also an enthusiastic purity to his actions, one that hasn't been replicated since.

What would Harry think of $38 seats in the bleachers and companies charging over a hundred bucks to watch from a rooftop? How would he feel about the scalping company that wheels around the neighborhood and sells its tickets from a giant Hummer? What would he say if a vendor charged him $5.50 for a beer? $4.25 for a hot dog?

We're capitalizing on Harry's wonderful creation, but doing little to honor it. And that's why I think Wrigleyville still sometimes feels like the first Christmas without Granddad. No one's sure how to put the angel atop the tree. No one's around to cut the turkey, just so.

I think about Harry and I miss him.

September 15–18—vs. St. Louis

Apart from the city's two newspapers, I find myself getting a lot of my Cubs news from message boards and blogs. The best happens to be *desipio.com*, a blog run by Andy Dolan, a Cubs fan from a small town in northern Illinois.

Desipio gained popularity in 2003 as the Cubs made their

charge to the playoffs. Now it's one of the biggest Cubs Web sites, getting over two million hits per month. Dolan's humor is no different than most guys my age. Taking a page from ESPN's Bill Simmons, he weaves pop culture references with his daily insights and link. The result is a bang-your-fist-on-the-table-funny take on the Cubs' players, manager and front office. Most of the jokes I've been using this season come from Dolan. He addresses the Cubs catcher as "Hank White" instead of his actual name, Henry Blanco. He refers to Jim Edmonds as "Lassie," claiming that the St. Louis center fielder has an unusual love for dogs. When announcer Chip Caray was in town, Dolan made sure to run a campaign so he would leave.

Along the way, Dolan has become influential. When Len Kasper got his broadcasting job, he contacted Dolan for a better view of the Cubs' fan psyche. A trade proposed on his site can quickly gather credibility in the eyes of many readers, despite the site's motto of "by idiots, for idiots."

Earlier in the year, I remarked on how there was a majority of fans who don't automatically accept every move the Cubs make. Dolan is the ringleader, questioning the moves of Dusty Baker and general manager Jim Hendry on a daily basis.

When I learned that Dolan was coming to Friday's game against the Cardinals, I knew I had to meet up with the man behind the monitor. And any doubts I had that he wouldn't show for a meaningless game in late September were erased with a post on his blog.

"I could just not go," Dolan wrote. *"I could 'vote with my feet,' so to speak. I don't go and that means several beers don't get sold that would if I'd gone, a couple hot dogs, maybe one of those hilarious 'boxing Cubs' doll things and those beads! Oh, how can you resist the beads!*

"I could sell my tickets. [But] I can't do this for several reasons. First, who's going to buy them? A Cardinals' fan, that's who. And I'll

be damned if I'm going to be responsible for letting two more of them into the park. They're going to be overrunning the place anyway, they won't be doing it in my seat."

The Cardinals opened the series last night, a Thursday, with a 6–1 win in the rain. Dolan has a little hope, though not much, for today's game. After driving over an hour to get to the stadium he meets me for lunch at—where else?—the Full Shilling.

We talk for almost two hours on topics ranging from Chip Caray to how he became a Cubs fan (like me, an early '80s trip to Wrigley). We also talk about one of his favorite targets, the White Sox, who are currently trying to hold off the Cleveland Indians in the AL Central.

"I've got a friend who's a Sox fan and he always points out that whenever he sees a 'special needs' person that he or she is almost always wearing a Cubs hat," Dolan says. "I just tell him that even *they* have enough sense not to root for the White Sox."

I ask Andy about being a Cubs fan. Does he like the pain and suffering that goes with it? Has he gotten used to it?

"You never get used to it," he says. "I've thought a couple of times about giving up and maybe rooting for someone else. But I'm scared that when I do that, they're finally going to win."

The Cubs go on to split the series, winning the second and last games of the four-game set. Wrigleyville is next to dead. On Sunday, as we walk to Subway for a Bears halftime snack, an SUV goes rolling by. A woman is hanging outside the window with the tickets.

"Do you want these?" she yells. "They're free!"

My friend and I shake our heads. Not today.

Chapter Seventeen

Closing Time

September 23–25—vs. Houston
September 27–28—vs. Pittsburgh

There's a little sadness as I walk down Clark Street for the last night game of the season. The Cubs have long been dead in the water, but it's still impossible not to hope for another month of the season. The weather is cold enough that I have to wear a sweatshirt, and the dusky chill evokes memories of the 2003 National League Championship series.

A little under two years ago, I was prowling these streets, crowded and noisy, rambunctious and hopeful. Outside the El station stood a man who had a sign looking for "just one." He was convinced he'd find the one Cub fan nice enough to sell him a ticket for face value. Steps away a broker was shouting to passersby that "all the cheap stuff, the three- and four-hundred-dollar tickets, is gone." Regular folk, done up in red and blue face paint, gathered on Waveland, forming a mob that couldn't follow the game except for scoreboard watching and an occasional pocket TV or radio. Inside, the stadium quaked when Kerry Wood hit a two-run homer to tie the game in the second, the most thrilling sporting moment I've ever seen live. And when Wood proceeded to give up seven earned runs—a performance that would leave him choking back postgame tears—everyone, inside and out, sat or stood in near silence.

That brief taste of October baseball in Wrigleyville proved to be a narcotic everyone associated with the team. It wasn't hard to see the mad aftereffects and the desperate actions of junkies looking for another fix. Sitting through a cold April day and rising for every 3–2 count was the perfect example of hope and desperation. Leaving a job in Kansas City was another.

That hope is all but gone now. I came back to watch the neighborhood again realize its fullest potential. The Cubs didn't fulfill their potential, and so we had no fuel for the fire. Things are back to normal and Wrigley is no longer a hot ticket or the cool thing to do. The line outside the Metro is longer for a band that 99.9 percent of the population has never heard of than for tickets outside Wrigley's main entrance. An hour ago, I desperately worked the phones looking for a tagalong partner for the game. Everyone declined. *"Go to the Cubs game? I don't know . . . it's kind of a good night for television."*

So, alone, I order my favorite combo at Wrigleysville Dogs—a soggy hot dog, a mess of fries, and root beer served in a foam cup—and settle into an orange seat. Wrigleysville Dogs is a pregame hangout for vendors, whose staging area is just south on Clark Street. As I eat, they stream in wearing green jerseys and royal blue hats, both made of mesh.

Four vendors sit at a table near the back. They're all in their mid-forties, the types of guys who look like they never enjoyed working a nine-to-five job. A vending job isn't going to set them up with a mansion in Barrington, but they like what they do. It gives them freedom that other jobs wouldn't. When the Cubs and Sox seasons are over, some of the guys will sell at Soldier Field or the United Center. But some of the beer guys make so much money that they get to take off a few months in the winter, one of the guys tells me.

These guys aren't beer vendors.

"You in the upper deck today?" one asks another.

"Yeah. Peanuts and pop. You?"

"Same. But lower deck."

One of the guys shuffles a deck of cards with one hand. Another tears a packet of mustard and applies it to a corn dog. Talk turns to the White Sox, who are two games ahead of the Indians in the AL Central. One of the vendors goes through a lengthy explanation of how the Sox can't possibly miss the playoffs because the Yankees and Red Sox must play each other three games this weekend, and so the wild card is almost all but guaranteed.

"Man, if the Sox can win the World Series, I won't have to work for a while," says one, referring to a preseason bet he placed on the Pale Hose.

"I wouldn't count on it," says his friend.

Thinking it will be easy to get a ticket to the bleachers, I approach a guy about my age who is displaying one of those "I've got extra tickets that I need to sell" expressions outside the gate on Waveland and Sheffield.

"Ten bucks for your extra?" I offer.

The seller, who's dressed like a member of the Young Republicans, manages to send a belittling scoff my way.

"I'll walk into the game with this ticket before I sell it for ten," he says.

Maybe he does not like my Puma sweatshirt and jeans.

I ask him if he's sure. "Ten bucks would get you two beers you wouldn't have otherwise."

"I have enough money for beer, thanks."

With that, Alex P. Keaton turns and walks toward the bleacher gate, shoving an unused ticket in the pocket of his Dockers to prove a point. You'd think a conservative-looking guy would have a good understanding of supply and demand. But so much for Chicago camaraderie. It's the first time all season that something unpleasant has happened with a fellow fan.

I find a ticket ten minutes later and wander into the bleachers. It's a semi-historical night. Beginning on Thursday, work will begin on the eighteen-hundred-seat expansion of the bleachers, the first major changes since the stands were erected in the late '30s. Perhaps not surprisingly, the Chicago media has virtually ignored the story, save for a column in the *Sun-Times* and some vague drawings that were released back in March. From that we learned that bleacherites will have access to the rest of the stadium, a never-before-bestowed privilege. And the standing room along the back walkway, where thousands of people have made friends along the fence, will be eliminated.

The other effects of the renovations are up for speculation. In right field, a teenager tells me that his uncle's demolition company will be handling the destruction of the bleachers and everything will be rebuilt up to the ivy-covered wall. Another guy says he's heard that the Cubs will be eliminating general admission free-for-all and switching to assigned seats. Everyone else around him shakes their heads. Surely the Cubs wouldn't go *that* far.

Then again, who knows? No one thought the Cubs would ever play a night game in Wrigley Field. No one thought there'd be a rotating advertising board behind home plate. If the Tribune Company figures it can make money by instituting a tiered pricing system in the bleachers, then we might be told where to sit in the bleachers.

The bleacher regulars aren't taking the renovations well. A group has printed up a batch of T-shirts, marking the demise of Chicago's favorite party place. "These Old Bleachers: 1937–2005," read the front of the shirts, with a choice of "left field," "center field," or "right field" printed on the back. In left field, a group hangs a black-lettered sign on the back left field fence:

"R.I.P. Bleachers."

After a few minutes, a security person requests that the sign come down.

For some Chicagoans, these bleachers are hallowed ground, more sacred than any place of worship. People laugh and cry together, and about more than just the Cubs. They attend each other's birthdays, weddings, and even funerals. To tamper with the atmosphere is to tear a valuable part of the city itself.

On the ramp to the bleachers, Jim sips an Old Style and ponders the changes. An accountant in his mid-forties, Jim has been sitting out here for twenty-five years. In a past life (the one without children, he says), he attended over forty games a season.

"How many do you make now?"

"The ones my wife knows about?" Jim says. "Around ten."

"Well, how many do you *actually* come to?"

"Let me see," says Jim, biting his lip. "About twenty or thirty."

"How is it possible your wife doesn't know?"

"Well, I work in the city," Jim says. "And I tell her I'm staying late and then come out to the night games. When it's over, I go back to the office and change. I only work a few El stops from here."

At this point, Jim grabs my notebook and scratches out his last name.

"The fact that I'm cheating on my wife with a baseball team will not be published," he says.

At this point, a buddy of Jim's stops by and jokingly claims they're half brothers. The truth is that they actually met in the bleachers in 1987 and have been friends since.

Jim's buddy leaves, claiming that he just promised to buy twenty beers for the people sitting around him. That leaves me alone with Jim again, so I ask him how he feels about the bleacher expansion.

"I look at it this way. . . . Baseball is a game of tradition and that, in turn, makes baseball fans traditional types of people. . . ."

Jim has been drinking.

"We want the fundamentals. We don't want the designated hitter. We don't want interleague play. We don't want unbalanced schedules where you play the fuckin' Pittsburgh Pirates eighty-four times a season. And we definitely don't want eighteen hundred more bleacher seats if that's going to mean big changes like getting rid of the walkway up there. Do you have any idea how many beers I've had while leaning up against that fence?"

My initial instinct is to agree with Jim. Human interaction will be cut down without the standing room in the back walkway. But at the same time—and cue the *Full House* music here—the bleachers are about the *people*, not the faded plastic benches themselves. The outfielders will still be within shouting distance. The guy next to you will still get up and crawl over you to the aisle fourteen times for beer and bathroom trips. Home runs from the opposition will still be rejected back onto the field.

Still, a concern remains: What are the renovations going to look like?

There's at least a bit of drama for the final night game of the season. Greg Maddux is starting, and he holds a 13–13 record. Two wins in his final two starts of the season will carry his streak of fifteen-win seasons to an unmatched eighteen. The media has been hyping this streak for the last half of the season, and while it's not going to boost ticket prices for the scalpers, at least it's something to watch for.

NASCAR legend Richard Petty throws out the first pitch, which leads to loud disapproval from the group behind me.

"What the hell does Richard Petty have to do with the Cubs?" roars the heckling ringleader. "Who's throwing tomorrow, Boris Yeltsin?"

Nomar hits a two-run homer in the bottom of the second inning, a left field blast that lands in the glove of Moe Mullins, who's watching the game from the stands. Mark Loiacano, the third-year Ballhawk, shakes his head at the veteran.

"I should have had that one," Loiacano says. "But Moe's good. He just beat thirty-six hundred people out here for that ball."

Through four innings, Maddux has a good shot at win number fourteen. But in the fifth, Pittsburgh left fielder Jason Bay hits a three-run homer to right, further cementing his reputation as a Cubs killer. Maddux goes all nine innings, but the Cubs fall 5–3.

"Look at it this way," says one fan as we head out of the bleachers and into the night for the last time in 2005. "Maddux has an eighteen-season streak of at least thirteen wins. That's still pretty damn good."

With the playoff chances dead and five games left in the season, optimism is still breathing at Wrigley Field.

"Wait 'Til Next Beer" reads the Miller Lite sign on Sheffield Avenue. In Wrigleyville, the next beer has already been served in the time it takes to read the sign. But next *year*, at least for the Cubs, is an estimated 186 days away. It's depressing to think about. Baseball is the only sport that delivers almost every day during the season, and after the next month it will disappear to leave only hot stove talk behind. And so it seems that I should breathe up today's entire experience and use it for those long winter nights when I've just dug the car out of a snowbank and the Bulls or Blackhawks aren't on television.

The weather for the season's final game at Wrigley is overcast. Neither warm nor chilly. There's a chance of rain, but nothing threatening in the immediate future.

Will and I are standing at the corner of Waveland and Kenmore. We've already picked up bleachers for ten bucks apiece and

272 • KEVIN KADUK

are watching the Ballhawks as they go through their final session of batting practice with the bleachers as we know them.

It's September 28 and the girls are still parading by in a variety of tight jeans and tighter tops. I sigh because these girls will soon disappear in the bulky leather coats, woolly mittens and scarves of a Chicago winter. It's depressing.

"Where do all these girls go in the off-season?" I ask aloud.

"You don't know about the spaceship?" Will asks.

"The spaceship?"

"My friend has a theory," he explains. "After the last home game, a spaceship comes down and all the hot Wrigley girls get into it and fly away. And next May, the spaceship will return and all the girls will come pouring out wearing short skirts and Cubs hats. It's the only explanation."

To our left, Andy Mielke is pulling down B.P. homers faster than anyone. Mike Diedrich, the Ballhawk documentarian, and his crew capture the whole scene on their cameras.

By the time the day is over, Mielke will pull down five baseballs, and while posing for a group picture on Waveland, he drops a few of them. Three months earlier, Mielke pledged this was his last season as a Ballhawk. He's sticking to his word and insists he doesn't feel one drop of sorrow.

"I've got bigger problems than the Cubs expanding the bleachers," he says. "This right here is just a hobby. It's just fun."

A few feet away, Ken Vangeloff owns up to feeling nostalgic.

"Am I sad? Not in the crying-my-eyes-out way of being sad," says Vangeloff, who is wearing an Indians hat in support of his favorite team. "But there is a certain sense of sadness in that this is the last day we'll be out here with Wrigley looking like this."

Vangeloff plans to come out to Waveland during the winter to check the progress of the bleachers expansion. He jokes (I think) that he'll be taking measurements of the wind and the height of the wall and applying physics to see if it'll be worth coming out next year.

Dave Davison says he'll be here either way.

"What else would I do?" he asks.

The turnstile clicks one last time for me this season. A bleacher usher is making fun of the guy who entered the park ahead of me. "He definitely had a bottle of something down his pants," the usher says. "Did you see him? He was walking like this."

The usher imitates a ginger waddle.

"He didn't want the bottle to fall out," he says.

Ten minutes before game time and the bleachers aren't close to being full. It looked the same way last night, but a late-arriving crowd filled the park close to capacity. Maybe it'll be the same way today.

A portion of the left field bleachers are roped off so that Len Kasper and Bob Brenly can broadcast the game from a different vantage point. It's a feature that Harry Caray perfected in the '80s, when he broadcasted shirtless from among the Bleacher Bums.

Kasper and Brenly are one season into their Cubs broadcasting careers and my jury is still out. Are they my favorites? No. Do they have potential? Maybe. Like I said before, sometimes it takes a while to warm up to the new guys. This is a good example.

The "R.I.P. Bleachers" sign is back on the left field fence, and security again comes to save the Tribune Company from any embarrassing propaganda.

"We don't allow signs on the back fence," the guard says.

"Like this one?" asks one fan, pointing to the WGN Sports sign hanging behind Kasper and Brenly. "Maybe we should take it down, too."

The guard says nothing before walking away.

Unlike last night, Wrigley Field remains half full, but it is a good crowd. The atmosphere seems like the last day of school, only we're not looking forward to a vacation from Wrigley. Still, those in the bleachers seem generally upbeat, and when Matt Murton turns and throws a ball to Bob Brenly, the crowd good-naturedly boos both of them.

"Hey, Brenly, give it up!" yells one man. "We paid to be out here."

In the front row of the bleachers, a man proposes to his girl-friend. A few seconds later, someone holds up a yellow sign with a drawing of a diamond ring. "She said yes!" it reads. Everyone applauds.

Mark Loiacano is in his usual spot in the left field bleachers, wearing his trademark camouflage pants and running between left and right field, depending on the batter. He shows me his glove, which has three fresh signatures from closer Ryan Dempster, reliever Will Ohman, and Murton, who has bolstered Cubs fans' hopes with a great end to the season.

"Ryan will always stop to talk [on Waveland] because I'm usually the first one out there," Loiacano says. "They called me over today and Will Ohman said, 'I've got a question for you. Do you have twelve pairs of camouflage pants? Or is it the same pair?' I told him I've been wearing these pants all season. That way they'd be able to recognize me."

My friend Haydn arrives, just having got off work at a downtown newspaper. We start buying each other beers, and Haydn announces that if the Cubs don't make significant improvements over the off-season, he'll no longer be coming to Wrigley Field.

"We can't just keep giving them money without getting anything in return," Haydn says. "This whole season was a joke. The stands are full every day and the Cubs don't even go .500 at home."

Haydn is right. Coming into today's game, the Cubs are

38–42 in their home park. Derrek Lee will later remark to the media that "it's odd . . . with so much fun and excitement here, it seems like you would play well here. But we didn't, so it's something that we need to get better at."

The Pirates take a 2–0 lead in the second inning when a throw by Nomar Garciaparra bounces off a runner's helmet and into right field. The play leads to two Pittsburgh runs, both unearned, off Mark Prior. The lead extends to 3–0 in the fifth, but Jose Macias leads off the bottom of the sixth with a solo homer to Waveland, the last homer to leave Wrigley in 2005. It lands, predictably, right in Andy Mielke's mitt.

"Macias?" is all Mielke can say.

Murton hits an RBI groundout later in the inning and Lee scores, bringing the score to 3–2.

A substantial rain, though not enough to make us seek shelter, comes in the eighth inning. By now we are sitting in the center field bleachers, high above the action. Two cute girls are behind us and we start to talk. Molly is still a big Corey Patterson fan and shushes Haydn when he starts heckling the underachieving center fielder. Brynn, Molly's freshman-year roommate from DePaul, is attending her first game at Wrigley, despite having lived in Chicago for over six years.

"It's great!" is Brynn's initial review.

Ohman, Roberto Novoa, and Michael Wuertz each pitch a scoreless inning of relief, giving the Cubs one final chance to send the fans home to winter with a victory and keep the team's chances alive for a third straight winning season, the first such streak in over thirty seasons.

The Cubs hitters respond, loading the bases with no outs. The rain is coming heavier, and the girls behind us both have soaked hair. Water drips off my Cubs hat and toward the ground. Ronnie Woo makes his final 2005 appearance in the bleachers. Holding his arms outstretched, he looks toward the field and holds the pose, like the famous *Cristo Redentor* statue overlooking Rio de Janeiro.

Patterson comes to the plate, and everyone manages a little groan except for Molly, who's certain her crush can come through in the clutch. Patterson is batting .218, the lowest Cubs average in recent memory. The Cubs would like for him to play in the winter Mexican League, but Patterson has balked at the suggestion, further estranging him from the fans.

But wouldn't a two-run single shut everyone up right about now?

Sure it would, but Patterson, as sure as this driving rain, strikes out and heads to the dugout in a shower of boos. Pinch hitter Ben Grieve comes to the plate, works a 3–2 count, and then swings at ball four, low and away, for out number two.

Jose Macias steps up to the plate, the last hope for the Cubs. But everyone knows how this story ends. Macias swings at a high pitch and pops it up toward second base for the final out of the home season.

There isn't much hand-wringing over the loss. This season was over long ago, but it would have been nice to see the Cubs off with a win. It didn't work out. What can you do? Shrug and head toward the exits, that's what.

See you next April.

The crowd spirals down the bleacher ramps and pours out onto the street, where the bucket drummers are keeping a cadence, charter buses are noisily waiting, and T-shirt vendors are trying to dump their stock for the year. Before I leave the gates, I pat a hand on the top of the entryway. I'll be back next April, but it's still a little sad.

Our group is soaked, but not ready to go home. In times like these, there can be only one solution. We head to Murphy's for a ceremonial final beer. I slap down some money on the bar and get a few beers in return.

"To next year," we toast.

We raise our plastic cups in the air.

Our hopes for the Cubs have hopped a train to next February and the promise of spring training. No doubt we'll catch up with them there.

Postscript

In the days after the season's final out, construction workers clogged Waveland and Sheffield, erecting tall wire fences and bringing in heavy machinery for the renovation of Wrigley's bleachers. The subsequent pounding of jackhammers proved to be a sufficient reminder that the Cubs were done for the season.

I passed Wrigley one afternoon on my way to the Lake Michigan bike path and saw the early damage. Like seeing a friend in a hospital bed, it was startling at first. The bricks of the outer left field wall had been removed, revealing the stadium's skeletal iron supports and the accumulated grime of almost seventy seasons of the bleachers.

A few feet away, I noticed that Dave Davison, one of the Ballhawks, was peeking through the fence's green fabric so he could get a better look. He had been out here since the start of the demolition, he told me, and planned to stay until the work was done. Dave had set up a few lawn chairs at the corner of Waveland and Kenmore and a few other onlookers were gathered around them.

I asked Dave if it hurt when he saw the initial demolition. He had, after all, spent the best portion of his life staring at a red-brick wall that had been turned into a pile of rubble. He shook his head.

"This is going to hurt the Cubs more than it hurts me," Dave said. "I don't think they realize what they're doing."

The demolition continued through October and by the end of the month, most of the bleachers had been torn down with only the ivy-covered outfield wall, the scoreboard and the upper portion of the center field seats left standing. Everything else was gone, making way for the bleacher improvements in 2006, for better or worse.

Perhaps not surprisingly, the city's newspapers paid little attention to the wrecking crew. Though editors at the *Tribune* always deny a bias toward pro-Cubs news, the absence of a story about opposition to the renovation was noticeable. That its parent company could proceed with a significant alteration to a beloved landmark without question was shocking. Had the changes been scheduled for the John Hancock Building, the Petrillo Music Shell, or the Adler Planetarium, there surely would have been a story in the city's larger newspaper.

But I had long since learned that being a Cubs fan means accepting the way the team is able to spin its image any way it wants. While positive spin seems beneficial for a Cubs fan, it can actually be a deterrent to the team's success. In 2005, 3,099,992 people saw a game at Wrigley Field, the second highest total in team history. And because all those people came out to see a 79–83 team the next question became, why should the Tribune Company try building a winner? It's an argument that Cubs fans have had among ourselves for some time now. Since no one's staying home when the Cubs are in town, it seems we're stuck with the situation.

As October wore on, another interesting story began to unfold. The crosstown White Sox, suffering an eighty-eight-year title drought of their own, began rampaging through the playoffs. First they took down Boston, three games to none, in the American League Division Series. Then, behind the strength of four straight complete games by the starting rotation, the White Sox defeated the Angels 4–1 in the ALCS, bringing the World Series to Chicago for the first time since 1959.

On a rainy Sunday night, I climbed to the upper deck at Sox Park with my dad and my brother for game two of the World Series. In the seventh inning, Paul Konerko hit an electrifying grand slam to left field. My dad reacted by jumping on me like he was twelve years old again. At that moment, moving back to Chicago became completely worth it.

The White Sox swept the Houston Astros in four games and the city of Chicago—or at least half of it—felt as if an enormous weight had been lifted from its shoulders. Two days after the clincher, over one million people crammed the downtown streets and welcomed home the Sox with a ticker tape parade. Chicago's championship drought was over, though not for the team that most had thought.

The reaction from Cubs fans was a mixed one. During game three, several women at the Full Shilling earnestly rooted for the Astros, despite the dirty looks and insults from some of the surrounding Sox fans. Will Byington, my photographer friend, took a different approach. Though he claimed to be strictly a Cubs fan, he cheered for the Sox during their playoff run, smartly identifying that it was about time the World Series trophy came to the great city of Chicago.

With the White Sox and Boston winning titles in consecutive years, the Cubs were left alone as the perpetual bridesmaid. Some said the Sox titles meant the Cubs would get theirs in '06, though a cynic would suggest their chance came in '03, when they blew it against the Marlins.

Either way, a new dynamic was scheduled to arrive in Wrigley in 2006 as the desperation for a World Series win grew. With the White Sox playing a smarter, tighter brand of baseball only eight miles away, Dusty Baker and his squad figured to face more criticism than ever.

The Indian summer ran long in Chicago and there were days in October, and even early November, when it seemed possible I could run over to Wrigley at the last minute and catch a game. Instead the area around the stadium had an eerie quality, like a once-grand hotel that had closed a few decades past. The mess by the bleachers didn't help things.

As winter neared, the Wrigleyville bars hunkered down to expect their usual trickle of business before gearing up again in March. Ronnie Woo could still be seen ambling along Clark Street, though not nearly as frequently. Chicago turned its eyes toward the Bears and the Bulls, but kept an eye on baseball's hot stove talk. Spring training was already only a few months away.

Meanwhile, I looked for something to fill my days. Namely, a job. I had a few options, though returning to a nine-to-five schedule after a season of freedom seemed less than appealing. At the final count, I attended sixty-two of the Cubs' eighty-one home games. Throw in fifteen Sox contests and a few games on the Eastern seaboard and my summer surely ranked among the all-time best. What fan wouldn't have wanted to be in my shoes for those five months?

In the end, my stunt was all about acting like baseball's version of Peter Pan. As for so many other people my age, gaining a footing in the real world proved to be a challenge. And though many would have accepted the change, I rebelled and tried to delay the aging process. I turned to the Chicago Cubs for a one-year reprieve and they delivered.

It's hard not to be happy when you're playing catch in the middle of Waveland or meeting a friend as she comes down the steps of the train station. Or making a new friend simply because he's sitting next to you, then turning to watch Mark Prior strike out ten in a complete-game shutout.

This book couldn't have been written about any other stadium. It's a lock that I'll attend hundreds of more Cubs games in the coming years. But none will have the meaning of a special summer when I celebrated my homecoming in the place I felt most comfortable.

As I prepared to face a winter of tall snowbanks, I prepared a virtual bank of memories to keep me warm. In this memory, I am walking down Waveland with a bag of peanuts in one hand and a radio in the other. It's ten minutes until game time and a gaggle of tank-topped girls smiles at me as they walk by. I enter Wrigley Field, drink two beers, eat two hot dogs and heckle the opposing right fielder from my bleacher seat in the third row. The Cubs win in the bottom of the ninth, and the sun is shining.

I dream about Wrigley, and everything seems possible.

Acknowledgments

It takes the right amount of (ill-advised?) encouragement to do something like leave your job to drink beer and watch the worst franchise in history for a season. For that, I thank my friends Rick Maese and Anna Roberts, whose prodding instant messages were the first to shove me off the cliff. This idea might not have left Kansas City if it weren't for them.

My agent, Greg Dinkin, showed great interest, calling me less than an hour after I e-mailed my proposal. For that (and the subsequent book deal), I am grateful. My editor, Mark Chait, took a chance on a young voice and provided great guidance throughout the entire process. He's one of the fastest e-mailers I know.

I've made a cottage industry of tweaking Kansas City, but I left behind dozens of great friends. *Star* sports editor Mike Fannin has always shown great enthusiasm for my writing, and he's one of the best developers of talent I know. Mike Fitzgerald was my Johnson County partner in crime, and despite our age difference, I consider him one of my best friends. Wright Thompson and Jeff Passan went through my initial drafts and gave me pointed comments. My only regret is that they weren't here to share more of my Wrigleyville mayhem. The entire staff in the *Star* sports department is too large to mention, but rest assured it's one of the best in the country. More important, they form a family-type environment at 1729 Grand, a rarity at a large metro.

To those in Chicago who reintroduced me to the neighborhood: Matt Sokol, Will Byington, Andy Mielke, Moe Mullins, Ken Vangeloff, Dave

Davison, Rich Buhrke and Mark Loiacano. Their devotion to the Cubs will be rewarded . . . hopefully someday soon.

Special thanks to Dan Alter, Joe Barnas, Jen Chen, Maggie Hessel-Mial, Katie Hollar and Derek Prater, Renee Metzler, Kristen Mochel, Chris Mc-Knight, Jonathan Phillips, Sledd Schultz, Patrick Whiting and Joe Wiermanski. All provided sympathetic ears during crabby bouts of writer's cramp and also proofed and critiqued several chapters. They rank among my best and most encouraging friends.

Also, for always humoring me (and for making me think my name had been legally changed to "How's the book?"): Jeff Agrest, Jeff and Emily Akin, Adam Anderson, Dan and Leslie Alter, Thea Basler, Shashank Bengali, Andy Bitter, Julie Bosman, Peter "Party Boy" Boylan, Haydn Bush, Micah Bycel, Brian Carlson, Tim Clavette, Mike Coyle, Johnny Daly, Colin Finan, Susan Fitzgerald, Jason Franchuk, Josh Fredericks, Marcus Fuller, Ben and Jill Goldsworthy, Julie Greschuk, Jeff Groves, Tom Ibarra, Nick Kowalczyk, Chris LeBarton, Kristee Logsdon, Bob and Mary Luder, Sam Mellinger, Trent Modglin, Mary Motzko, Jenny Oliver, Nicole Poell, Ron Pollack, Manu Raju, Allyson Ross, Anitra Rowe and Dan Schulte, Derek Samson, Jamie Schaller, Frank and Jenni Schwab, Jay Senter and Julia Westhoff, Damon Smith, Laura Sterchi, Christopher Tennant, Art and Angie Wachholz and Colleen Wheeling.

And finally—to my wonderful parents, to the brother and sister that always make me proud, to my unconditionally loving grandparents, to my fantastic cousins, to my saintly aunts, and to my three uncles who are all named Chuck—it's not always easy loving someone who's perpetually yelling at the television. And yet somehow you do it.

October 2005